Volume 2
25 Patchwork Quilt Blocks

Dedication

To Warren, Grace, and Leo. Thank you for putting up with the mess and cereal for dinner while I chase my dreams. I love you.

25 Patchwork Quilt Blocks Volume 2
© 2014 by Katy Jones

Martingale®
19021 120th Ave. NE, Ste. 102
Bothell, WA 98011-9511 USA
ShopMartingale.com

Printed in China
19 18 17 16 15 14   8 7 6 5 4 3 2 1

Library of Congress Cataloging-in-Publication Data is available upon request.

ISBN: 978-1-60468-427-8

Mission Statement

Dedicated to providing quality products and service to inspire creativity.

Credits

PRESIDENT & CEO: Tom Wierzbicki

EDITOR IN CHIEF: Mary V. Green

DESIGN DIRECTOR: Paula Schlosser

MANAGING EDITOR: Karen Costello Soltys

ACQUISITIONS EDITOR: Karen M. Burns

TECHNICAL EDITOR: Laura Stone Roberts

COPY EDITOR: Melissa Bryan

PRODUCTION MANAGER: Regina Girard

ILLUSTRATOR: Adrienne Smitke

COVER & TEXT DESIGNER: Connor Chin

PHOTOGRAPHER: Brent Kane

Contents

Introduction

Welcome to the follow-up to my first book, *25 Patchwork Quilt Blocks* (Martingale, 2013). In this book I bring you a whole new collection of 25 blocks that mix traditional designs, modern interpretations of historical blocks, and entirely new blocks. The blocks will gently introduce you to using templates, basic machine appliqué, and rotary cutting and machine piecing simple shapes such as squares and triangles. Then you'll be invited to try slightly more complicated techniques, such as hand appliqué and English paper piecing. There's nothing here that should cause fear; just start at the beginning and work your way through the blocks, or pick randomly from those that appeal to you the most. Then be inspired to use your favorite block or blocks in a larger project, be it an apron, a bag, or a quilt.

Each block is 6" finished (meaning that the block measures 6" square after it's sewn into a project), without a border. With all the blocks, you have the option of sewing on a border that increases the finished size to 8"—which makes sewing the block into a finished quilt top or other project all the more easy! The blocks are designed to use small pieces of fabric or scraps and to be absolutely beginner-friendly.

Quilting is not a cheap hobby. You could buy a quilt from any department store for far less than you'll spend making a quilt from start to finish (taking all your costs into consideration). But, if you're reading this, you have already decided you don't want to buy quilts from a store and would rather have something you can say you made yourself. You might have seen all of the beautiful quilts on blogs or other social-networking sites, or maybe you've been reading quilting magazines. Don't feel despondent if your first efforts aren't quite perfect. Everyone has to start somewhere, and no one has an award-winning first quilt. No one. You might have seen pictures of peoples' fabric stashes and been blown away by the amount of beautiful fabrics they own. Building up a stash takes a whole heap of time and (more importantly) money. Most quilting stores offer bundles of fabrics cut into manageable sizes that are perfect for starting out and will help you build a nice stash. Buy a fabric because you love it, not just because it was on sale or a great deal. That "really great deal" fabric will sit unused on a shelf somewhere for a very long time.

I hope that the patchwork in these pages will inspire you and that this book continues you on a quilting journey that lasts your lifetime. Enjoy yourself. Have fun. Let your personality shine through in the quilts you make, and they'll be all the better for it. Don't sweat the mistakes; don't let them defeat you. It took you a long time as a child to learn to run—so take the baby steps and savor them, even when you trip and fall flat on your face. If you were still a child, you'd jump straight back up, dust yourself off, and carry on. And know this: there really is nothing more satisfying than climbing into bed and pulling a freshly laundered quilt around you that you made yourself.

The Basics

Pages and pages could be devoted to the fundamentals of quilting, but I wanted to keep this book slim and light while packing it with as many inspirational projects as possible. With that said, I have included a section on English paper piecing (see page 6), since a few of the blocks and two of the projects call for this specific technique; but you can find info about all the basics—from rotary cutting right through binding a quilt—in handy, free, downloadable form at ShopMartingale.com/HowtoQuilt. The how-to guides are really wonderful and will give you every piece of information you need to get started. Save them, print them, and refer to them often as you make your way through this little book.

If you're just starting on your quilting journey, there are a number of items that you really cannot live without. You may already own some of these items if you are a regular sewist, but others are specific to quilting, and without them you'll find the task quite difficult. I've kept the shopping list as small as it can possibly be, because some of the equipment can get expensive, but all of these items are absolute must-haves.

Sewing Machine

A sewing machine is essential and should have the following features:

> Patchwork or ¼" presser foot, to help you achieve the perfect ¼" seam allowances required in most patchwork.

> Dual-feed feature (available on many machines) or walking foot to feed multiple layers of fabric through the machine easily, reducing the likelihood of puckering or bunching in your quilt.

> Darning foot, which is useful for free-motion quilting.

> Ability to drop or cover the feed dogs, which are the jagged bits that sit under your machine foot and feed the fabric through the machine. When free-motion quilting, you will need to override the action of the feed dogs.

When shopping for a sewing machine, buy the best you can afford. It's far better to have a machine that you can grow into than one you'll quickly grow out of. Fancy stitches are not necessary; for the most part, you'll really only use a straight stitch and a zigzag stitch. Try, try, try before you buy—get a feel for the machine, and never finalize your purchase without taking it for a "test drive"! Oil and clean your machine as instructed by the manufacturer, change the needle often, and look after your machine as if it were a child!

Rotary Cutter, Rulers, and Cutting Mat

A rotary cutter is a very sharp round blade with a handle. When used with a quilter's ruler and cutting mat, the rotary cutter gives you precise and clean-cut fabric pieces. A 45 mm rotary cutter is the most useful, along with a ruler that is 6" x 24" or 6½" x 24" and a self-healing cutting mat that's 18" x 24" or larger. (Buy the biggest you can fit on your table—you cannot have a mat that is too big!) Craft stores and quilting shops often carry sets that include a mat, cutter, and ruler. In addition to the crucial 24"-long ruler, you will find a myriad of other ruler shapes and sizes available—but the one you will need most of all is the long one. For the purposes of this book, a 6½" or 8½" square ruler is handy for trimming and squaring up your blocks, but not essential.

Scissors

You will need a pair of sharp, good-quality dressmaking shears that you use strictly for fabric, as well as a smaller pair of scissors, such as embroidery scissors or snips, for trimming threads.

Pins

You can buy quilting pins specifically designed for patchwork and quilting, but any pins will work as long as they are sharp. Don't sew over a pin—it can break the needle and damage your sewing machine!

You may also want to use basting pins, which are safety pins with a slight curve. They are easy to poke through the multiple layers of a quilt sandwich, holding things in place during the machine-quilting process.

Fabric

High-quality 100% cotton quilting fabrics are much better than trying to use different types of fabrics (such as corduroy, silk, voile, velveteen, and so on) or low-quality fabrics. This is especially true when you are first starting out. Cotton quilting fabrics are produced specifically for quilting, and buying good-quality fabric reduces the risk of a disaster, such as color running, unusual shrinkage, or fading. Prewash and iron your fabrics to reduce the risk of colors bleeding in your final project, and store your fabrics away from direct sunlight.

Batting

Many types of batting are available, and you should try a variety before committing to a favorite. My personal preference is a cotton-polyester mix that has a little shrinkage and is low loft (thin) to give a better drape.

Natural fibers shrink when washed, so if you like that antique, crinkled look, go for a natural fiber. Those wrinkles can help hide those little mistakes we all make when starting out, such as slightly mismatched points or less-than-perfect quilting! However, if you prefer minimal crinkles, try a polyester fiber. And if you plan to make multiple quilts and store them folded, a polyester or polyester-blend batting will resist creasing.

Batting is also available in different lofts, or weights—the higher the loft, the thicker the batting. Thick batting can be tricky to quilt; it's puffy, so it doesn't result in the flat look that you may be used to seeing in shop samples or on your favorite blogs. A high-loft polyester batting might be the cheapest option in your local store, but that doesn't mean it should be your first choice—the old adage "you get what you pay for" is so true. Just as with fabric, buying good-quality batting designed for quilting is a must. If you are making pot holders, oven mitts, or anything else that needs to withstand high heat, you will need to buy a special insulated batting. Never think you'll be OK using regular batting for a pot holder—you'll burn your hands the first time you use it! (I can speak from experience!)

Needles

Sewing-machine needles come in a variety of sizes and types. The ones you'll use the most are a size 80/12 universal needle for piecing and a size 90/14 quilting needle for machine quilting.

Thread

A good-quality thread is essential. Sewing machines sometimes have a preference as to which they like best. My own sewing machine loves one particular brand of thread better than any other. Until you are familiar with your machine, don't go crazy and buy up all the thread you see. Start with one thread and try it out thoroughly. Use it for a whole project, check the way it feels in your project, and see how the stitches lie. Do they pull? If so, refer to the manual that came with your machine, follow the trouble-shooting process to adjust the thread tension, and try again. Finding a thread that your machine likes and that you like the look of is an important step and shouldn't be rushed.

It's considered best practice to use a cotton thread when piecing cotton fabrics. Good habits start at the very beginning, so buy the best you can afford. Premium cotton thread is smooth and generates a low amount of lint (the fuzz that builds up as you sew). You don't need a whole library of colors—white, black, off-white, and gray are your essentials.

Iron

Most likely you already have an iron. If your iron gets hot and has a steam function, that's all you need. (You can use a spray bottle and water if your iron doesn't have a steam function.)

English Paper Piecing

This technique is a personal favorite of mine and I'm always working on one English paper-pieced project or another. It's completely portable, so it's perfect when you're riding along on car journeys, sitting by the pool in the summer, or watching TV in the evening. This centuries-old method hasn't changed since its birth. Even as sewing technology and tools continue to advance, English paper piecing remains the same—paper templates, fabrics, a needle, and thread.

Basting Straight-Edged Shapes

Trace the number of shapes required for the pattern you are using onto copier paper or old envelopes and cut out on the drawn lines. (This technique is great for using up junk mail!)

1 Pin a paper template to the wrong side of your fabric. Cut the fabric at least ¼" larger than the template on all sides. It doesn't need to be a perfect match to the shape; you can even start with a fabric square to save time.

2 Fold one edge of the fabric over the template, and then fold the next edge over the first to form a mitered fold. Using a hand-sewing needle and knotted thread, take two stitches through the fold to hold the folded fabric in place. Stitch only through the fabric, not through the paper template as well. This will make removing the papers later so much easier! (If you're used to stitching through the fabric *and* the paper, give this method a try. You'll be surprised at the accuracy of your

seam allowance and at the amount of time you save with this method.)

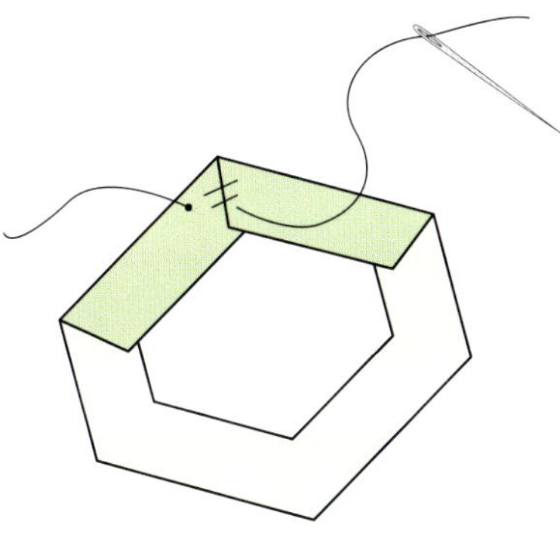

3 Keeping the seam allowance folded tightly around the template, fold the next fabric edge over the template, move to the next corner, and take a backstitch through the folds. Gently snug up your thread until the folds lie flat, but the papers aren't bent.

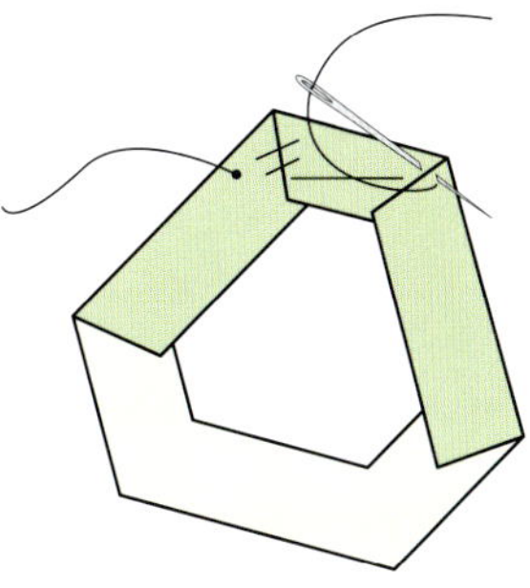

4 Continue around until you have secured each corner, and then take a couple of backstitches in the last fold and snip your thread, leaving a 1" to 2" tail. Repeat until you have basted all the shapes you need.

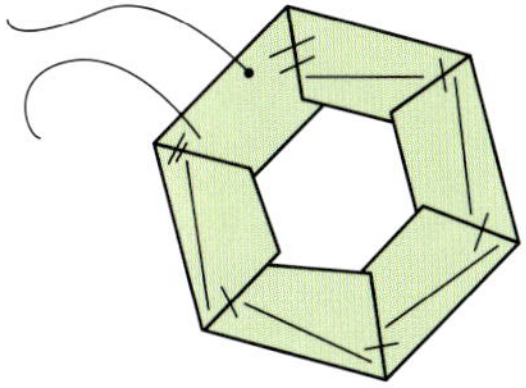

Use a paper clip, basting clip, or similar item to hold the paper and seam allowances tight at the first corner and keep the fabric from slipping.

Basting Shapes with Sharp Angles

Use the same technique as before, but at sharp points "let the tails wag," meaning to allow the excess seam allowance to overhang the point. The seam allowances will form a little tail that will be hidden when the shapes are sewn together in the finished piece.

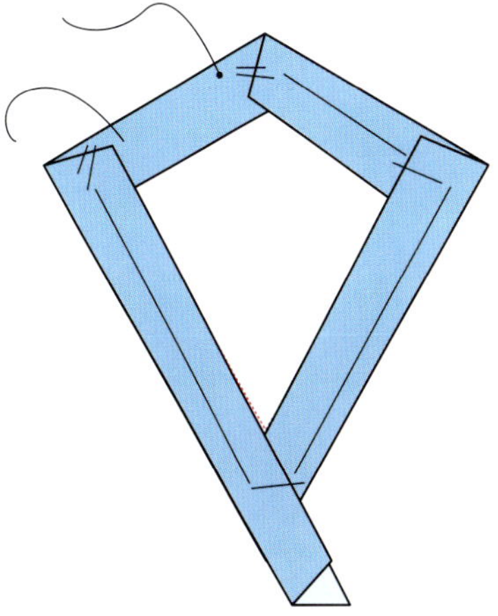

Sewing Prepared Shapes Together

Using a high-quality cotton thread, cut a length of thread approximately as long as your forearm. Prepare the thread with beeswax or a thread conditioner to prevent knots. When sewing your pieces together, start with a knotted thread and backstitch to secure. At the end of every side or seam, secure the corners by taking two stitches together.

Place two of the basted shapes right sides together and with edges aligned. Whipstitch across the edges, catching both fabrics but not the paper template. Work on making approximately 8 to 10 stitches per inch. If you make your stitches too close together, you'll form a ridge that will be visible and unattractive on the front of your work . . . not to mention that it'll take you forever! Your stitches should be pulled taut and even, but not too tight. Repeat this process until all of your shapes are sewn together as instructed in the pattern you're using.

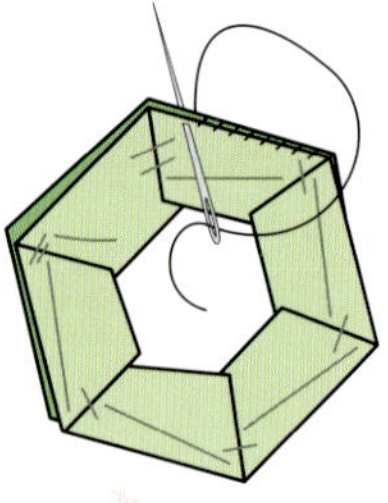

Removing the Papers

Once you have finished your block and all edges are secured (either by being sewn to another patch or block, or by being appliquéd in place), you can remove the papers. Simply pull the paper templates out—there's no need to remove the basting stitches, as they're hidden on the wrong side of the patchwork. (If you basted through both fabric and papers, you'll need to remove the basting before you can remove the papers.) If you are appliquéing onto a background, as with the blocks in this book, then remove only the papers at the center of each piece (the ones that are secured by another shape). Leave the papers in the patches around the perimeter of the appliqué until you have appliquéd the piece onto the background. They'll be removed later.

Appliquéing onto a Background

Pin the pieced motif onto the background fabric using short appliqué pins; they're less likely to cause tangles in your thread, and your fingers will thank you when they're not constantly stabbed with long pins! Pin from the center outward, making sure that each edge is smooth and lying flat.

Start at any point of the pinned motif and take very small slip stitches every ⅛" or so around the entire perimeter of the paper-pieced motif. Make sure you catch the background fabric in each stitch and avoid sewing through the papers. This method is exactly the same for the Grandmother's Flower block (page 31), the English Paper-Pieced Heart block (page 32), and the Daisy Dresden Plate block (page 35).

Removing the Remaining Papers

Carefully cut away the background fabric beneath the appliqué, keeping at least ¼" to the *inside* of the appliquéd motif's edge. Use small scissors and be very careful not to cut through the appliqué. Remove the papers and press your finished block.

Block 1
Boxed In

Materials

4 squares, 2" x 2", of gray background print

4 rectangles, 2" x 3½", of brown print

1 square, 3½" x 3½", of focal print (center a chosen motif from the print within the square)

Optional border:

2 strips, 1½" x 6½"

2 strips, 1½" x 8½"

Block Instructions

1 Sew brown rectangles to opposite sides of the focal-print square. Press the seam allowances toward the square.

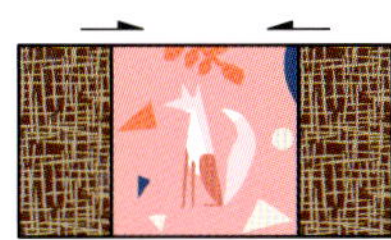

2 Sew a gray square to each end of the remaining brown rectangles. Press the seam allowances toward the squares.

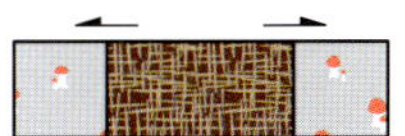

Make 2.

3 Lay out the three rows as shown and sew together. Press the seam allowances away from the center row.

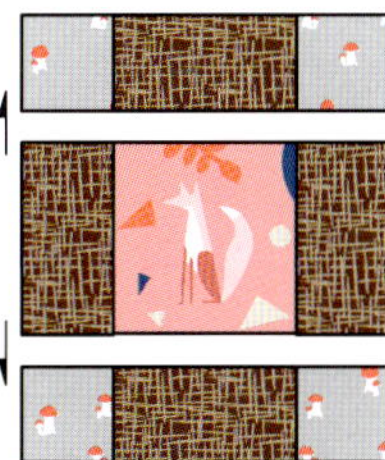

4 To add the optional border, sew the shorter strips to opposite sides of the block, pressing the seam allowances toward the strips. Then join the longer strips to the remaining two sides of the block. Press the seam allowances toward the strips.

Block 2
Square in a Square

Materials

1 square, 3½" x 3½", of focal print

2 rectangles, 2" x 3½", of white-and-red polka dot

2 strips, 2" x 6½", of white-and-red polka dot

Optional border:

2 strips, 1½" x 6½"

2 strips, 1½" x 8½"

Block Instructions

1 Sew the polka-dot rectangles to the top and bottom of the gray square. Press the seam allowances toward the rectangles.

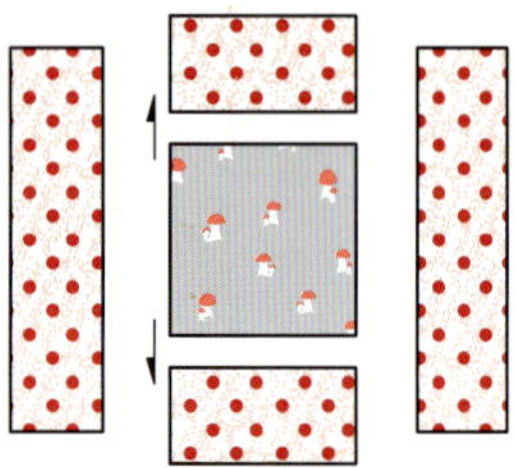

2 Sew the polka-dot strips to the remaining two sides of the square. Press the seam allowances toward the strips.

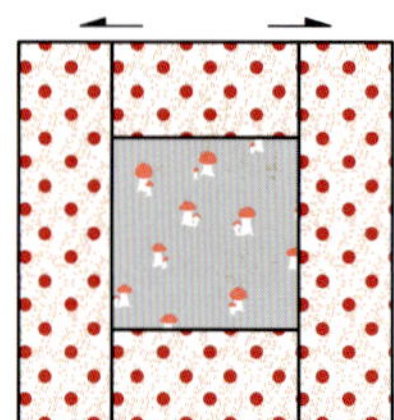

3 To add the optional border, sew the shorter strips to opposite sides of the block, pressing the seam allowances toward the strips. Then join the longer strips to the remaining two sides of the block. Press the seam allowances toward the strips.

Block 3
Circles and Squares

Materials

- 4 squares, 2" x 2", of red print
- 4 rectangles, 2" x 3½", of light background print
- 1 square, 3½" x 3½", of blue print
- 1 strip, 2½" x 6½", of multicolored print
- 1 strip, 2½" x 6½", of paper-backed fusible web

Optional border:

- 2 strips, 1½" x 6½"
- 2 strips, 1½" x 8½"

Block Instructions

1 Using the pattern on page 37, trace three 2" circles, including the center line, onto the paper side of the fusible web. Following the manufacturer's instructions, press the fusible web to the wrong side of the multicolored strip. Cut out the circles on the outer line. Cut two of the circles in half on the drawn center line.

2 Sew light rectangles to opposite sides of the blue square. Press the seam allowances toward the square.

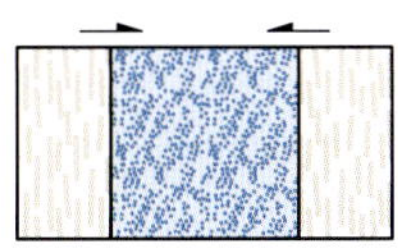

3 Sew a red square to each end of the remaining light rectangles. Press the seam allowances toward the squares. Make two.

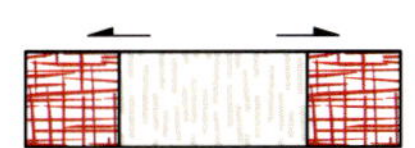

Make 2.

4 Lay out the three rows as shown and sew together. Press the seam allowances away from the center row. Fuse the full circle to the center of the block. Fuse a half circle to the center edge of each side of the block.

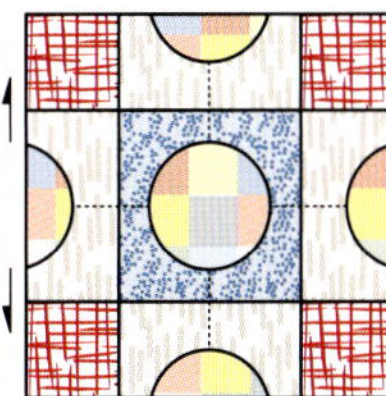

5 Using a straight stitch, carefully sew close to the edge of each fused shape.

6 To add the optional border, sew the shorter strips to opposite sides of the block, pressing the seam allowances toward the strips. Then join the longer strips to the remaining two sides of the block. Press the seam allowances toward the strips.

Block 4
Pinwheel

Materials

2 squares, 4" x 4", of light background print; cut in half diagonally to yield 4 triangles

1 square, 4" x 4", *each* of 4 assorted prints; cut in half diagonally to yield 8 triangles (4 will be extra)

Optional border:

2 strips, 1½" x 6½"

2 strips, 1½" x 8½"

Block Instructions

1 Join a light triangle to an assorted-print triangle along their long edges to make a half-square-triangle unit. Press the seam allowances open to reduce bulk. Repeat to make one unit from each of the four assorted prints. Trim the units to measure 3½" x 3½".

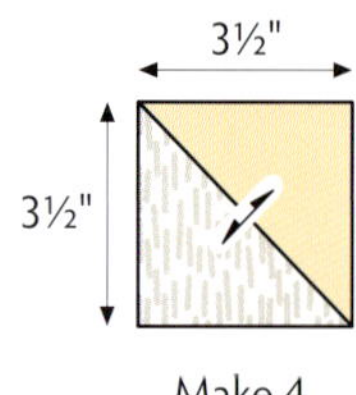

Make 4.

2 Lay out the half-square-triangle units in two rows as shown. Sew the units into rows and press the seam allowances open to reduce bulk.

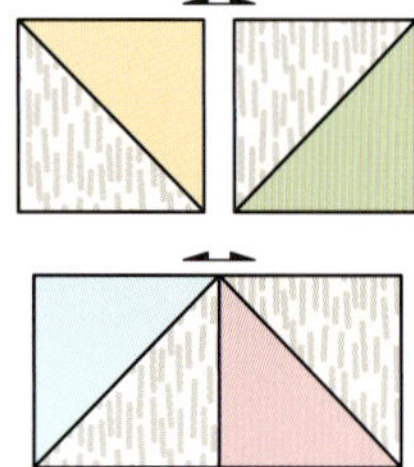

3 Sew the rows together and press the seam allowances open to reduce bulk.

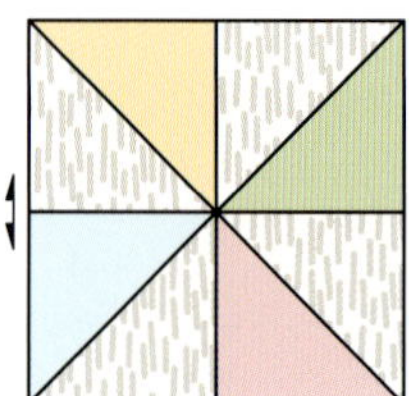

4 To add the optional border, sew the shorter strips to opposite sides of the block, pressing the seam allowances toward the strips. Then join the longer strips to the remaining two sides of the block. Press the seam allowances toward the strips.

Block 5
Cotton Reels

Materials

2 squares, 3½" x 3½", of light background print

1 square, 4" x 4", *each* of 4 assorted prints; cut in half diagonally to yield 8 triangles (4 will be extra)

Optional border:

2 strips, 1½" x 6½"

2 strips, 1½" x 8½"

Block Instructions

1 Join two assorted-print triangles along their long edges to make a half-square-triangle unit. Press the seam allowances open to reduce bulk. Make two. Trim the units to measure 3½" x 3½".

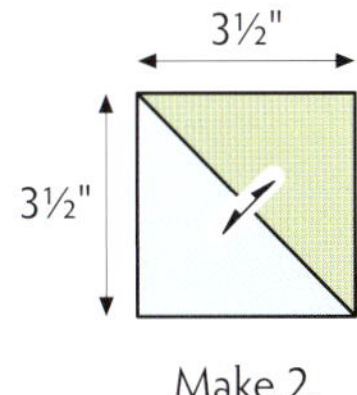

Make 2.

2 Lay out the half-square-triangle units and the background squares as shown and sew into rows. Press the seam allowances open to reduce bulk.

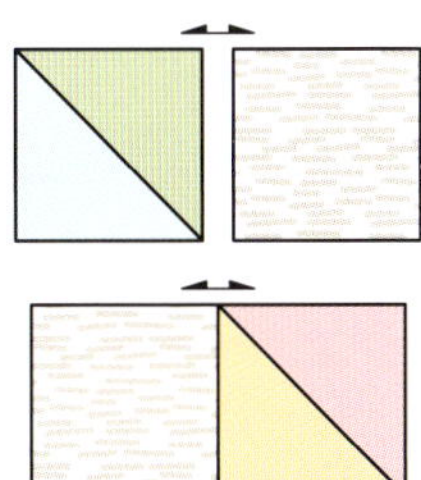

3 Sew the rows together and press the seam allowances open to reduce bulk.

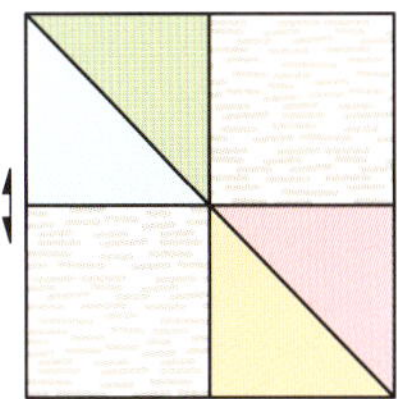

4 To add the optional border, sew the shorter strips to opposite sides of the block, pressing the seam allowances toward the strips. Then join the longer strips to the remaining two sides of the block. Press the seam allowances toward the strips.

Block 6
Double Square

Materials

1 square, 4" x 4", of red print
1 square, 4" x 4", of blue print
2 squares, 4" x 4", of large-scale black-and-white polka dot

Optional border:
2 strips, 1½" x 6½"
2 strips, 1½" x 8½"

Block Instructions

1 Draw a diagonal line on the wrong side of the blue square. Layer the square on a polka-dot square, right sides together, and stitch ¼" on each side of the marked line. Cut the squares apart on the drawn line to make two half-square-triangle units. Press the seam allowances open to reduce bulk. Trim the units to measure 3½" x 3½". Repeat using the red square and the remaining polka-dot square to make two more half-square-triangle units.

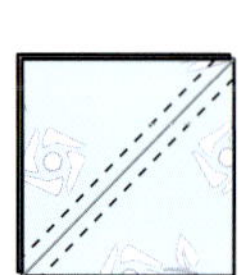 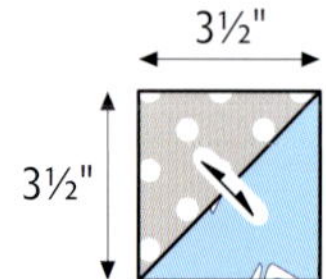 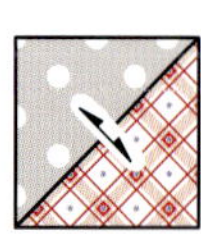

Make 2 of each.

2 Lay out the half-square-triangle units as shown and sew into rows. Press the seam allowances open to reduce bulk.

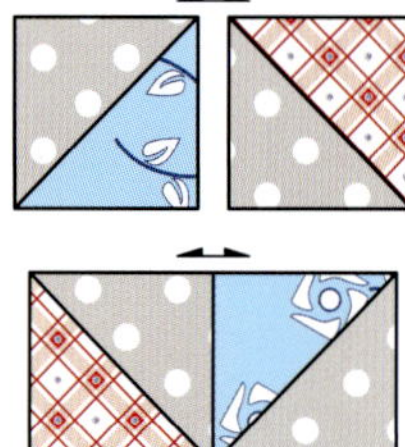

3 Sew the rows together and press the seam allowances open to reduce bulk.

4 To add the optional border, sew the shorter strips to opposite sides of the block, pressing the seam allowances toward the strips. Then join the longer strips to the remaining two sides of the block. Press the seam allowances toward the strips.

Block 7
Little House

Materials

- 1 strip, 2½" x 6½", of light-blue background print
- 1 square, 3" x 3", of light-blue background print
- 1 square, 3" x 3", of black print
- 1 square, 2½" x 2½", of black print
- 1 square, 2½" x 2½", of brown print
- 2 squares, 2½" x 2½", of focal print (center a chosen motif from the print within each square)

Optional border:

- 2 strips, 1½" x 6½"
- 2 strips, 1½" x 8½"

Block Instructions

1 Draw a diagonal line on the wrong side of the light-blue square. Layer the square on the black 3" square, right sides together, and stitch ¼" on each side of the marked line. Cut the squares apart on the drawn line to make two half-square-triangle units. Press the seam allowances open to reduce bulk. Trim the units to measure 2½" x 2½".

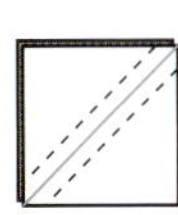
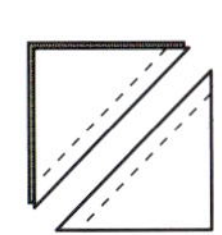
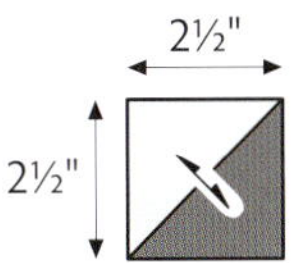

Make 2.

2 Lay out the light-blue strip, the half-square-triangle units, and the black, brown, and focal-print 2½" squares in three rows as shown. Sew the pieces into rows. Press the

seam allowances as indicated by the arrows to create opposing seams.

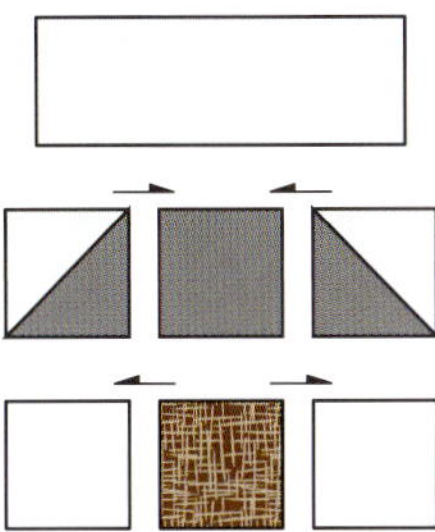

3 Sew the rows together and press the seam allowances away from the center row.

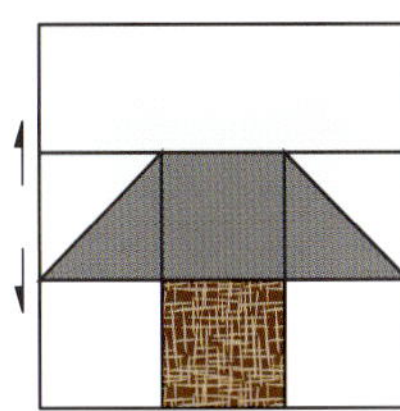

4 To add the optional border, sew the shorter strips to opposite sides of the block, pressing the seam allowances toward the strips. Then join the longer strips to the remaining two sides of the block. Press the seam allowances toward the strips.

Block 8
Cheats Geese

Materials

- 3 squares, 3" x 3", of black-and-white background print
- 3 squares, 2½" x 2½", of black-and-white background print
- 1 square, 3" x 3", *each* of 3 assorted prints or solids

Optional border:

- 2 strips, 1½" x 6½"
- 2 strips, 1½" x 8½"

Block Instructions

1 Draw a diagonal line on the wrong side of the assorted print or solid 3" squares. Layer each square on a black-and-white 3" square, right sides together, and stitch ¼" on each side of the marked line. Cut the squares apart on the drawn line to make six half-square-triangle units. Press the seam allowances open to reduce bulk. Trim the units to measure 2½" x 2½".

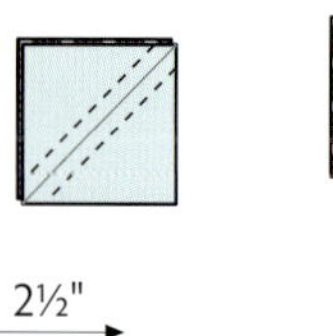

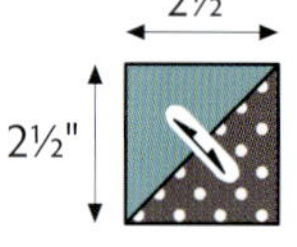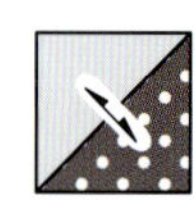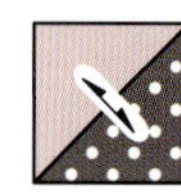

Make 2 of each.

2 Lay out the half-square-triangle units and the 2½" squares in three rows as shown. Sew the pieces into rows. Press the seam allowances as indicated by the arrows to create opposing seams.

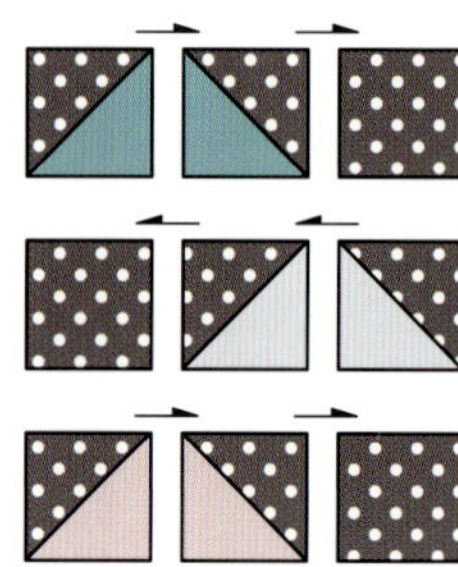

3 Sew the rows together and press the seam allowances toward the center row.

4 To add the optional border, sew the shorter strips to opposite sides of the block, pressing the seam allowances toward the strips. Then join the longer strips to the remaining two sides of the block. Press the seam allowances toward the strips.

Block 9
Ziggity Zag

Materials

5 squares, 3" x 3", of black-and-white back-ground print; cut in half diagonally to yield 10 triangles (1 will be extra)

6 squares, 3" x 3", of assorted prints and solids; cut in half diagonally to yield 12 triangles (3 will be extra)

Optional border:

2 strips, 1½" x 6½"

2 strips, 1½" x 8½"

Block Instructions

1 Select nine assorted triangles and join each one to a black-and-white triangle along their long edges to create nine half-square-triangle units. Press the seam allowances open to reduce bulk. Trim the units to measure 2½" x 2½".

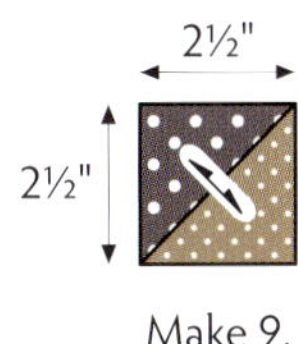

Make 9.

2 Lay out the half-square-triangle units in three rows as shown. Sew the pieces into rows. Press the seam allowances as indicated by the arrows to create opposing seams.

3 Sew the rows together. Press the seam allowances open to reduce bulk.

4 To add the optional border, sew the shorter strips to opposite sides of the block, pressing the seam allowances toward the strips. Then join the longer strips to the remaining two sides of the block. Press the seam allowances toward the strips.

Block 10
Eccentric Star

Materials

- 4 squares, 3" x 3", of black-and-white background print
- 4 squares, 3" x 3", of red print
- 1 square, 2½" x 2½", of red print

Optional border:

- 2 strips, 1½" x 6½"
- 2 strips, 1½" x 8½"

Block Instructions

1 Draw a diagonal line on the wrong side of the red 3" squares. Layer each square on a black-and-white square, right sides together, and stitch ¼" on each side of the marked line. Cut the squares apart on the drawn line to make eight half-square-triangle units. Press the seam allowances open to reduce bulk. Trim the units to measure 2½" x 2½".

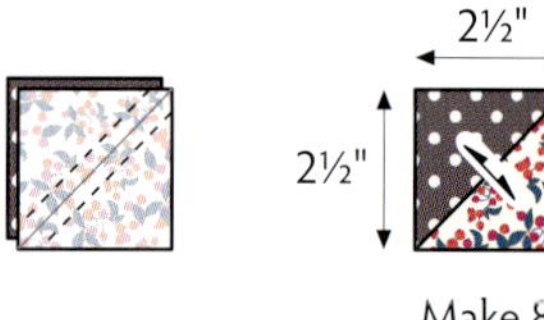

Make 8.

2 Lay out the half-square-triangle units and the 2½" square in three rows as shown. Sew the pieces into rows. Press the seam allowances as indicated by the arrows to create opposing seams.

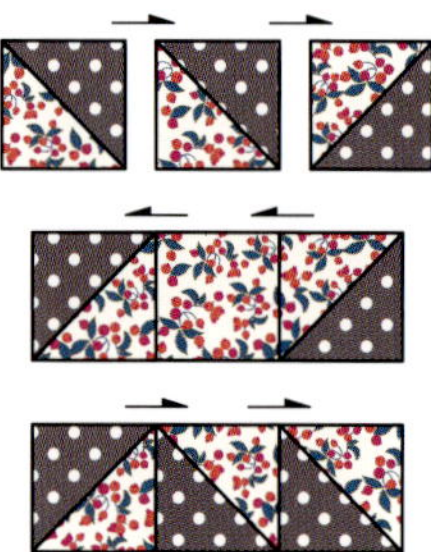

3 Sew the rows together. Press the seam allowances open to reduce bulk.

4 To add the optional border, sew the shorter strips to opposite sides of the block, pressing the seam allowances toward the strips. Then join the longer strips to the remaining two sides of the block. Press the seam allowances toward the strips.

Block 11
Sawtooth Star

Materials

4 squares, 2" x 2", of light background print

4 squares, 2½" x 2½", of light background print

4 squares, 2½" x 2½", of red print

1 square, 3½" x 3½", of focal print

Optional border:

2 strips, 1½" x 6½"

2 strips, 1½" x 8½"

Block Instructions

1 Draw a diagonal line on the wrong side of the light 2½" squares. Layer each square on a red square, right sides together, and stitch ¼" on each side of the marked line. Cut the squares apart on the drawn line to make eight half-square-triangle units. Press the seam allowances open to reduce bulk. Trim the units to measure 2" x 2".

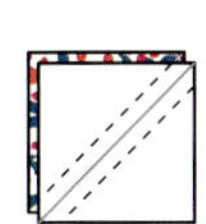 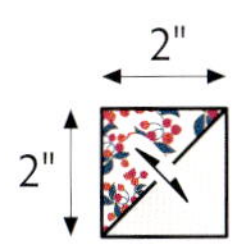

Make 8.

2 Sew two half-square-triangle units together as shown. Press the seam allowances open to reduce bulk. Repeat to make a total of four units.

Make 4.

3 Lay out the units from step 2, the light 2" squares, and the focal-print square in three rows as shown. Sew the pieces into rows.

Press the seam allowances as indicated by the arrows to create opposing seams.

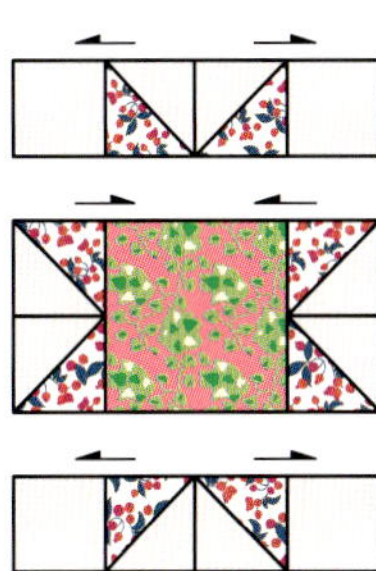

4 Sew the rows together. Press the seam allowances open to reduce bulk.

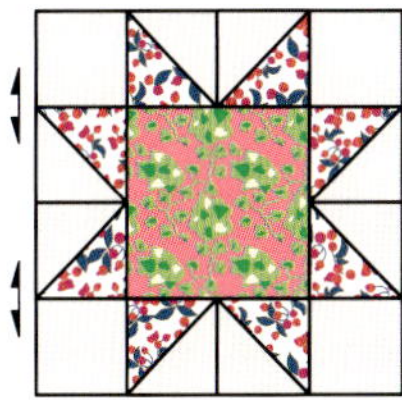

5 To add the optional border, sew the shorter strips to opposite sides of the block, pressing the seam allowances toward the strips. Then join the longer strips to the remaining two sides of the block. Press the seam allowances toward the strips.

Block 12
X Marks the Spot

Materials

8 squares, 2½" x 2½", of gray background print

1 square, 3½" x 3½", *each* of 4 assorted red prints

Optional border:

2 strips, 1½" x 6½"

2 strips, 1½" x 8½"

Block Instructions

1 Draw a diagonal line on the wrong side of the gray squares. Position a marked square on one corner of a red 3½" square, right sides together. Sew on the marked line. Trim the excess corner fabric, leaving a ¼" seam allowance. Flip the corner triangle open and press the seam allowances open to reduce bulk. Repeat on the opposite corner of the red square. Make four units.

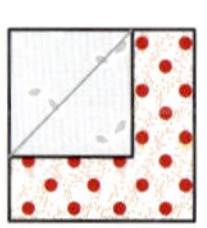 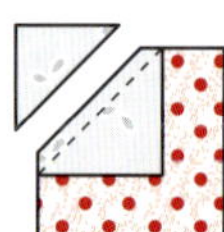 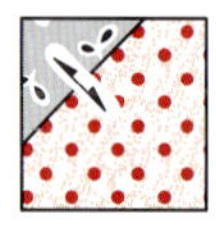

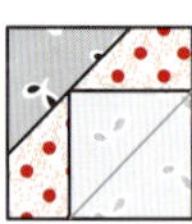 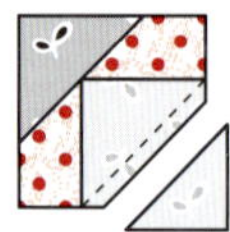 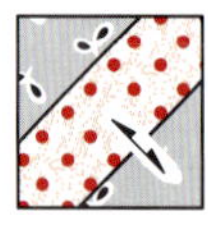

Make 4.

2 Lay out the four units in two rows as shown. Sew the units into rows. Press the seam allowances as indicated by the arrows to create opposing seams.

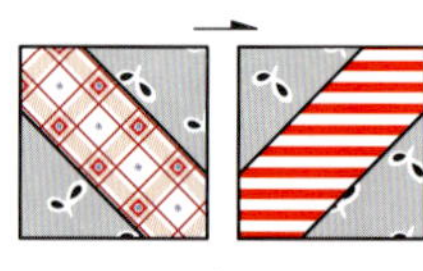

3 Sew the rows together and press the seam allowances open to reduce bulk.

4 To add the optional border, sew the shorter strips to opposite sides of the block, pressing the seam allowances toward the strips. Then join the longer strips to the remaining two sides of the block. Press the seam allowances toward the strips.

Block 13
Petals

Materials

9 squares, 2½" x 2½", of assorted beige prints

9 rectangles, 1½" x 3½", of assorted bright prints

Paper-backed fusible web

Optional border:

2 strips, 1½" x 6½"

2 strips, 1½" x 8½"

Block Instructions

1 Using the pattern on page 37, trace nine petals onto the paper side of the fusible web. Roughly cut out the petals, leaving about ¼" margin around the outline. Following the manufacturer's instructions, fuse a petal to the wrong side of each bright rectangle. Cut out the petals exactly on the marked line.

2 Sew the nine beige squares into three rows as shown. Press the seam allowances open to reduce bulk.

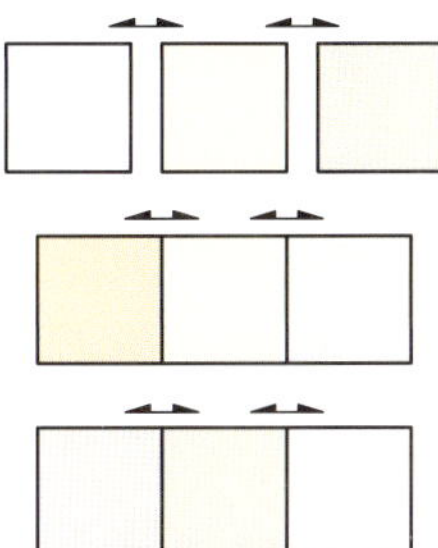

3 Sew the rows together. Press the seam allowances open to reduce bulk.

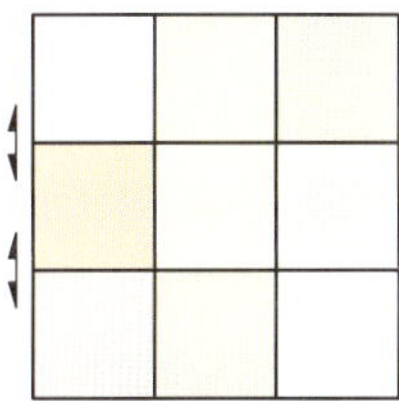

4 Remove the paper backing from the petals and arrange them on the beige squares, referring to the diagram and the photo for placement guidance. Fuse the petals in place. Machine straight stitch close to the edge of each petal to secure.

5 To add the optional border, sew the shorter strips to opposite sides of the block, pressing the seam allowances toward the strips. Then join the longer strips to the remaining two sides of the block. Press the seam allowances toward the strips.

Block 14
Paper Pinwheels

Materials

2 squares, 2½" x 2½", of black-and-white background print

8 squares, 2" x 2", of black-and-white background print

2 squares, 2½" x 2½", of light print

1 square, 3½" x 3½", of turquoise-and-yellow polka dot

Optional border:

2 strips, 1½" x 6½"

2 strips, 1½" x 8½"

Block Instructions

1 Draw a diagonal line on the wrong side of the light squares. Layer each square on a black-and-white 2½" square, right sides together, and stitch ¼" on each side of the marked line. Cut the squares apart on the drawn line to make four half-square-triangle units. Press the seam allowances open to reduce bulk. Trim the units to measure 2" x 2".

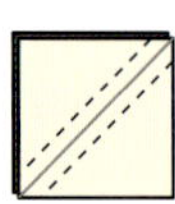 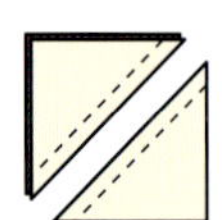 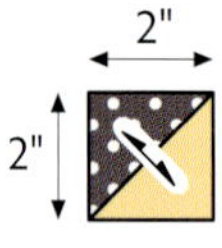

Make 4.

2 Lay out the black-and-white 2" squares, the half-square-triangle units, and the 3½" polka-dot square as shown. To make the center row, join the half-square-triangle units and black-and-white squares into pairs first, and then sew them to the sides of the polka-dot square. Sew the remain-

ing pieces into two rows as shown. Press all seam allowances as indicated by the arrows.

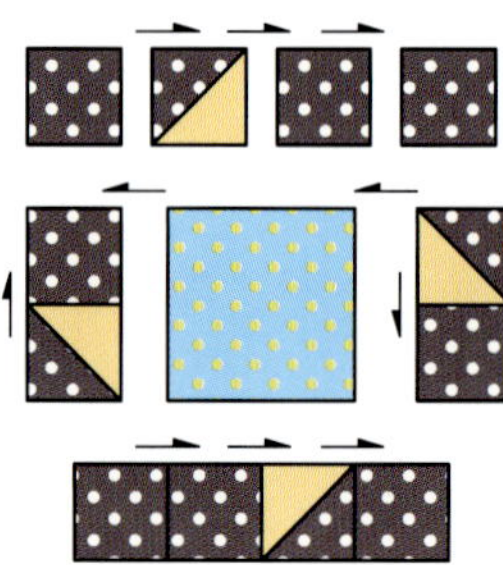

3 Sew the rows together. Press the seam allowances as indicated by the arrows.

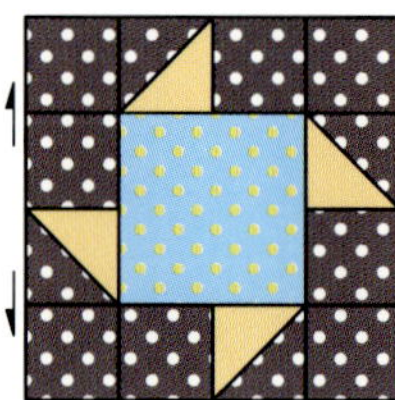

4 To add the optional border, sew the shorter strips to opposite sides of the block, pressing the seam allowances toward the strips. Then join the longer strips to the remaining two sides of the block. Press the seam allowances toward the strips.

Block 15
Brick Wall

Materials

3 squares, 2½" x 2½", of black-and-white
  background print

1 rectangle, 2½" x 4½", *each* of 3 assorted
  prints

Optional border:

2 strips, 1½" x 6½"

2 strips, 1½" x 8½"

Block Instructions

1 Join a black-and-white square to a print
rectangle and press the seam allowances
toward the square. Make three units.

 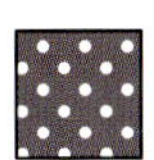 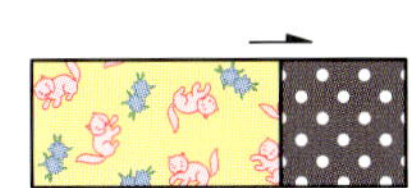

Make 3.

2 Arrange and sew the units together as
shown. Press the seam allowances open to
reduce bulk.

3 To add the optional border, sew the shorter
strips to opposite sides of the block, pressing the seam allowances toward the strips.
Then join the longer strips to the remaining two sides of the block. Press the seam
allowances toward the strips.

"

Block 16
Slice of Pie

Materials

1 square, 3½" x 3½", *each* of 4 assorted background fabrics

1 square, 4" x 4", of green print

1 square, 4½" x 4½", of red-and-white polka dot

1 square, 4" x 4", of paper-backed fusible web

1 square, 4½" x 4½", of paper-backed fusible web

Optional border:

2 strips, 1½" x 6½"

2 strips, 1½" x 8½"

Block Instructions

1 Using the patterns on page 37, trace circle A, including the center lines, onto the paper side of the fusible-web 4" square. Repeat with circle B and the 4½" square of fusible web. Roughly cut out the circles, leaving about ¼" margin around the outline. Following the manufacturer's instructions, fuse circle A to the wrong side of the green square. Fuse circle B to the wrong side of the polka-dot square. Cut out the circles exactly on the marked lines. Cut the circles into quarters on the drawn center lines.

2 Remove the paper backing and position one green and one red quarter circle onto opposite corners of a background square. Fuse the quarter circles in place. Using a straight stitch, carefully stitch close to the edge of each fused shape. Make a total of four fused squares.

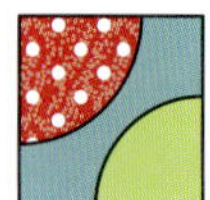

Make 4.

3 Lay out the fused squares in two rows as shown. Join the pieces into rows and press the seam allowances open to reduce bulk.

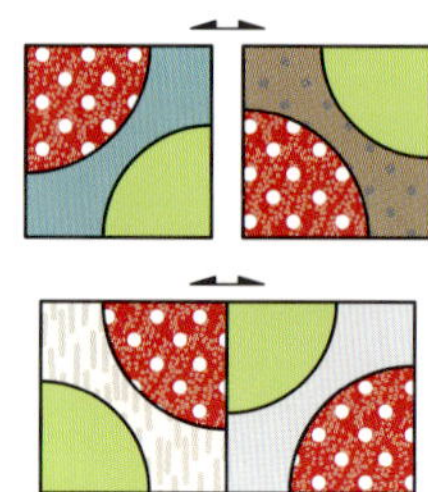

4 Sew the rows together and press the seam allowances open to reduce bulk.

5 To add the optional border, sew the shorter strips to opposite sides of the block, pressing the seam allowances toward the strips. Then join the longer strips to the remaining two sides of the block. Press the seam allowances toward the strips.

Block 17
Windblown

Materials

8 squares, 2½" x 2½", of light background print

4 squares, 2½" x 2½", of black print

4 squares, 2½" x 2½", of red-and-white polka dot

Optional border:

2 strips, 1½" x 6½"

2 strips, 1½" x 8½"

Block Instructions

1 Draw a diagonal line on the wrong side of four light squares. Layer each square on a black square, right sides together, and stitch ¼" on each side of the marked line. Cut the squares apart on the drawn line to make eight half-square-triangle units. Press the seam allowances open to reduce bulk. Repeat, using the red squares and the remaining light squares to make eight more half-square-triangle units. Trim the units to measure 2" x 2".

 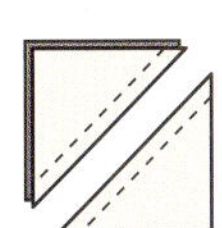 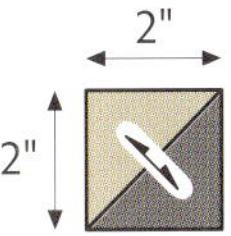 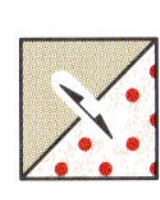

Make 8 of each.

2 Lay out two light-and-black units and two light-and-red units in two rows as shown. Join the pieces into rows and press the seam allowances open to reduce bulk. Make two of these quadrants. Use the remaining units, in reversed positions, to make two more quadrants. Press the seam allowances open to reduce bulk.

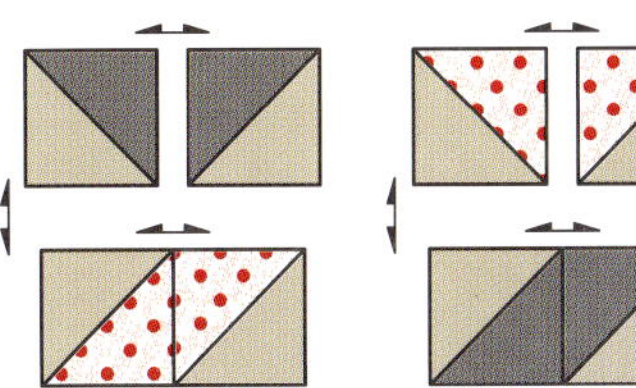

Make 2 of each.

3 Lay out the quadrants in two rows as shown. Sew the quadrants into rows. Press the seam allowances open to reduce bulk.

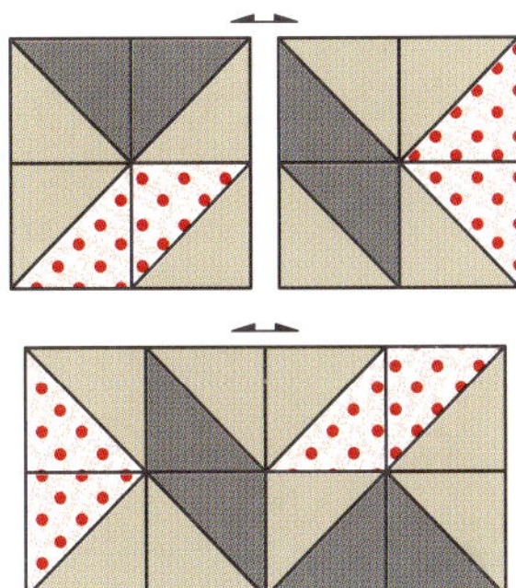

4 Sew the rows together. Press the seam allowances open to reduce bulk.

5 To add the optional border, sew the shorter strips to opposite sides of the block, pressing the seam allowances toward the strips. Then join the longer strips to the remaining two sides of the block. Press the seam allowances toward the strips.

Block 18
Spinning Star

Materials

6 squares, 2½" x 2½", of brown background print

6 squares, 2½" x 2½", of red-and-white polka dot

1 square, 3½" x 3½", of focal print

Optional border:

2 strips, 1½" x 6½"

2 strips, 1½" x 8½"

Block Instructions

1 Draw a diagonal line on the wrong side of the polka-dot squares. Layer each square on a brown square, right sides together, and stitch ¼" on each side of the marked line. Cut the squares apart on the drawn line to make 12 half-square-triangle units. Press the seam allowances open to reduce bulk. Trim the units to measure 2" x 2".

  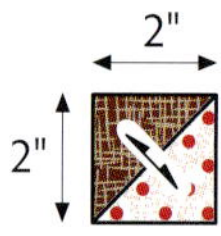

Make 12.

2 Lay out the half-square-triangle units and the focal-print square as shown. To make the center row, join the half-square-triangle units into pairs first, and then sew them to the sides of the focal-print square. Sew the remaining pieces into two rows as shown. Press all seam allowances open to reduce bulk.

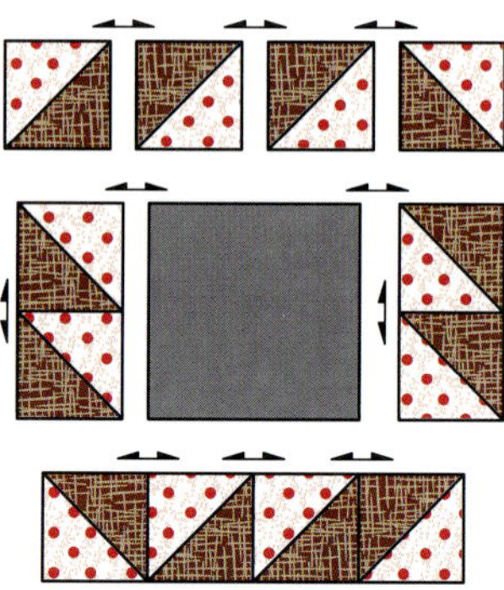

3 Sew the rows together. Press the seam allowances open to reduce bulk.

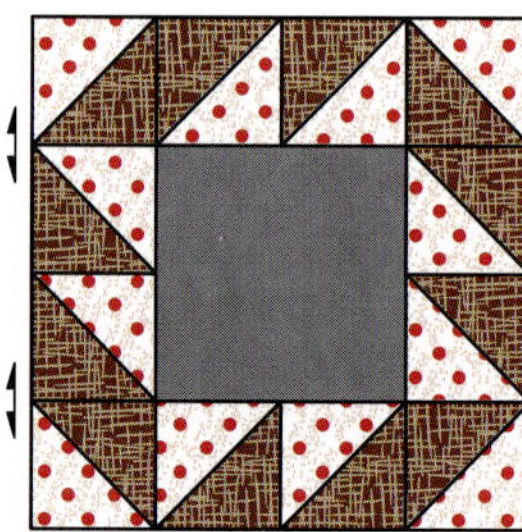

4 To add the optional border, sew the shorter strips to opposite sides of the block, pressing the seam allowances toward the strips. Then join the longer strips to the remaining two sides of the block. Press the seam allowances toward the strips.

Block 19
Right Hand of Friendship

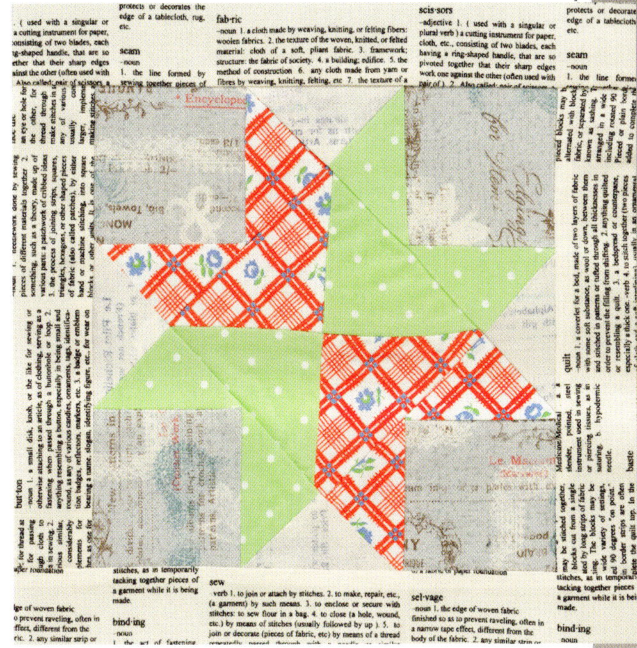

Materials

1 square, 3¼" x 3¼", of light background print; cut into quarters diagonally to yield 4 triangles

4 squares, 2½" x 2½", of light background print

1 square, 3¼" x 3¼", of green-and-white polka dot; cut into quarters diagonally to yield 4 triangles

1 square, 2⅞" x 2⅞", of green-and-white polka dot; cut in half diagonally to yield 2 triangles

1 square, 3¼" x 3¼", of red print; cut into quarters diagonally to yield 4 triangles

1 square, 2⅞" x 2⅞", of red print; cut in half diagonally to yield 2 triangles

Optional border:
2 strips, 1½" x 6½"
2 strips, 1½" x 8½"

Block Instructions

1 Join a green-and-white 3¼" triangle to a light 3¼" triangle with their short edges aligned and the green-and-white triangle on top. Make two pieced-triangle units. Press the seam allowances open to reduce bulk. Repeat with the light triangle on top to make two more pieced-triangle units.

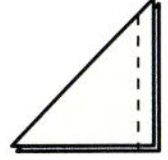 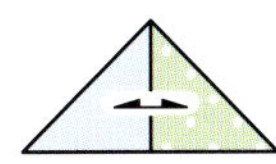 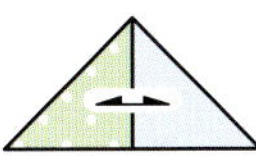

Make 2 of each.

2 Join pieced triangles to two adjacent sides of a light 2½" square as shown to make a large triangle unit. Press the seam allowances open to reduce bulk. Make two.

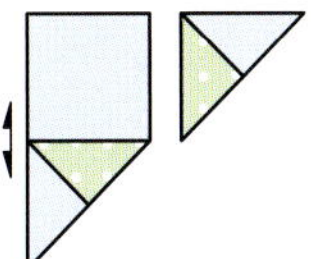 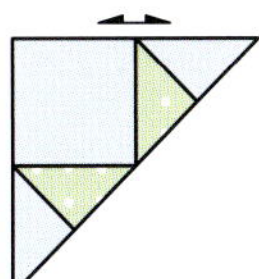

Make 2.

3 Sew red 3¼" triangles to two adjacent sides of a light 2½" square. Press the seam allowances open. Make two.

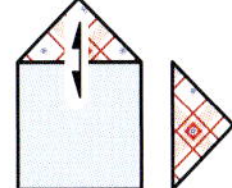 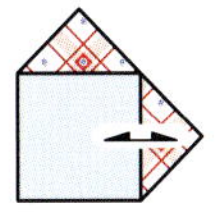

Make 2.

4 Join a green-and-white 2⅞" triangle to a red 2⅞" triangle with their short edges aligned and the green-and-white triangle on top. Make two and press the seam allowances open. Join these two units to

make an hourglass unit. Press the seam allowances open.

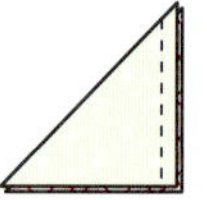 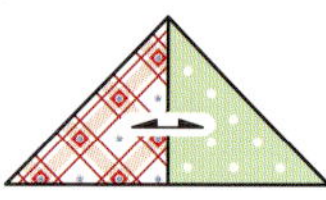

Make 2.

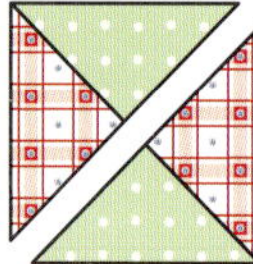 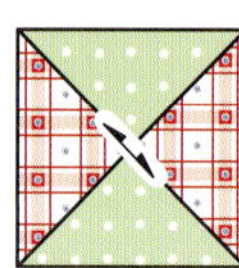

5 Lay out the two large triangle units, the two units from step 3, and the hourglass unit as shown. Sew the two units from step 3 to the red sides of the hourglass to make a diagonal row. Press the seam allowances open. Join the two large triangle units to

the diagonal row to complete the block. Press the seam allowances open.

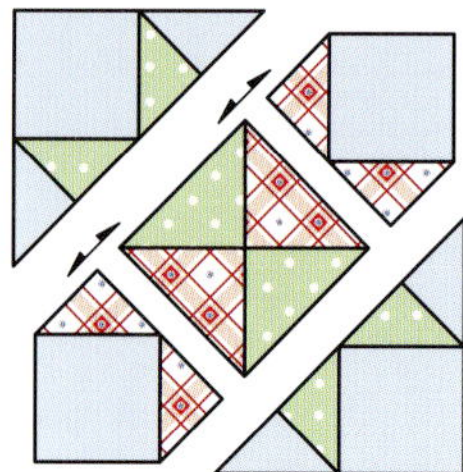

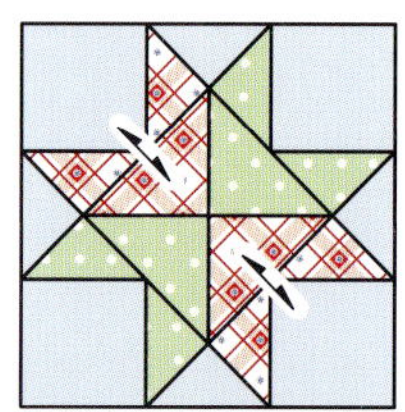

6 To add the optional border, sew the shorter strips to opposite sides of the block, pressing the seam allowances toward the strips. Then join the longer strips to the remaining two sides of the block. Press the seam allowances toward the strips.

Block 20
String Block

Materials

40 strips, 1" to 1½" wide x at least 6" long, of assorted bright prints (you may have strips left over)

4 squares, 4" x 4", of copier paper

Optional border:

2 strips, 1½" x 6½"

2 strips, 1½" x 8½"

Block Instructions

1 With right sides together, lay two bright strips diagonally across the center of a paper square. Make sure the strips are long enough to cover the edges of the paper square. Using a ¼" seam allowance, sew the strips to the paper.

2 Flip the top strip open and finger-press the seam allowances to one side. Continue adding strips in the same manner and finger-pressing as you go.

 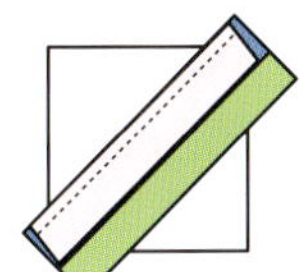 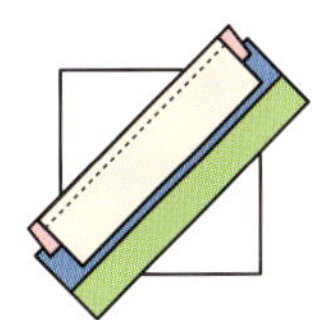

3 When half of the paper is completely covered, turn the paper around and, working from the center strip, continue to add strips until the paper square is completely covered. Press with a *dry* iron. Repeat with the remaining paper squares.

4 With the paper side up, trim the squares to measure 3½" x 3½".

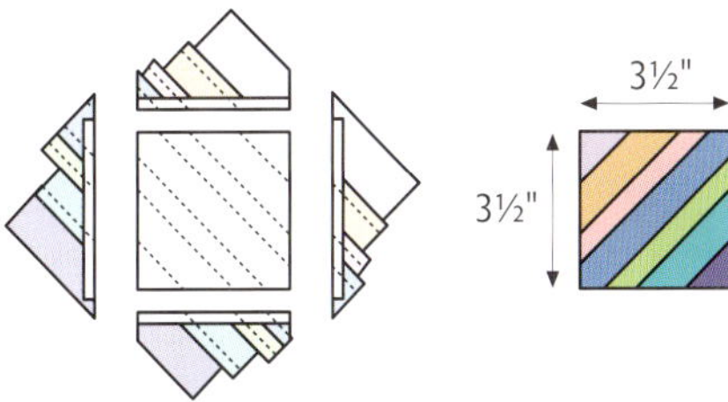

5 Lay out the trimmed squares in two rows as shown. Sew the squares into rows. Press the seam allowances open to reduce bulk. Sew the rows together. Press the seam allowances open.

6 To add the optional border, first stitch ⅛" from the block edges to stabilize the bias edges. Then sew the shorter strips to opposite sides of the block, pressing the seam allowances toward the strips. Join the longer strips to the remaining two sides of the block. Press the seam allowances toward the strips.

Block 21
Framed Diamond

Materials

- 1 square, 2½" x 2½", of focal print
- 2 strips, 1" x 2½", of green plaid
- 2 strips, 1" x 3½", of green plaid
- 2 strips, 1" x 3½", of blue solid
- 2 strips, 1" x 4½", of blue solid
- 2 squares, 4½" x 4½", of red print; cut in half diagonally to yield 4 triangles

Optional border:

- 2 strips, 1½" x 6½"
- 2 strips, 1½" x 8½"

Block Instructions

1. Sew the green plaid 2½" strips to the sides of the focal-print square. Press the seam allowances toward the strips. Sew the plaid 3½" strips to the top and bottom. Press the seam allowances toward the strips.

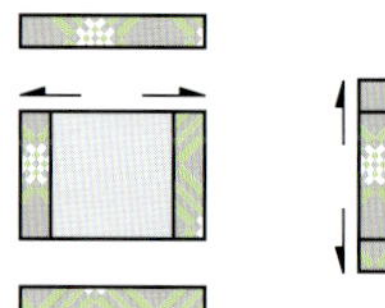
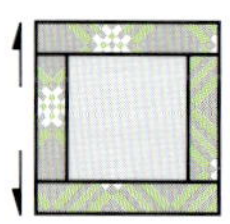

2. Sew the blue 3½" strips to the sides of the unit from step 1. Press the seam allowances toward the strips. Sew the blue 4½" strips to the top and bottom to complete the center unit. Press the seam allowances toward the strips.

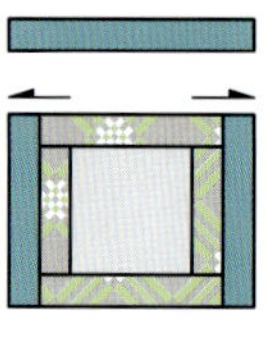
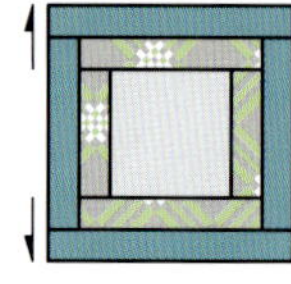

3. Center and sew red triangles to opposite sides of the center unit. Press the seam allowances toward the triangles. Center and sew red triangles to the remaining two sides to complete the block. Press the seam allowances toward the triangles. Trim the block to measure 6½" x 6½", making sure to keep the center unit centered. You should have ⅛" of red showing beyond the points of the blue square.

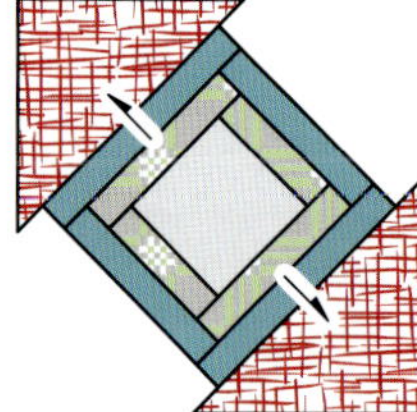
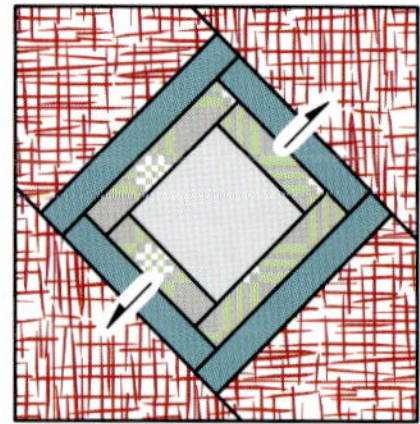

4. To add the optional border, sew the shorter strips to opposite sides of the block, pressing the seam allowances toward the strips. Then join the longer strips to the remaining two sides of the block. Press the seam allowances toward the strips.

Grandmother's Flower

Materials

- 1 square, 2½" x 2½", of white print
- 1 square, 2½" x 2½", *each* of 6 assorted green prints
- 1 square, 6½" x 6½", of black background fabric
- Paper for hexagons

Optional border:

- 2 strips, 1½" x 6½"
- 2 strips, 1½" x 8½"

Block Instructions

1 Refer to "English Paper Piecing" on page 6 when making this block. Using the large hexagon pattern on page 37, trace and cut out seven paper hexagons. Pin a hexagon template to each 2½" square and trim the fabric around the hexagon, leaving at least ¼" on all sides for the seam allowance. Baste the white and green pieces around the paper hexagons. Make seven.

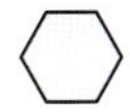 

Make 1.   Make 6.

2 Whipstitch one green hexagon to the white hexagon. Add a second green hexagon by whipstitching it first to the green hexagon already in place, and then whipstitching it to the white hexagon as indicated by the arrows. **Note:** If you bend the first green hexagon in half when sewing the second green hexagon to the white one, it will be easier to align the hexagons.

3 Continue to add green hexagons in a ring around the white hexagon. When adding the last hexagon to the ring, stitch three sides to the adjoining hexagons as shown.

4 Center the hexagon flower on the background square, pin, and hand stitch in place.

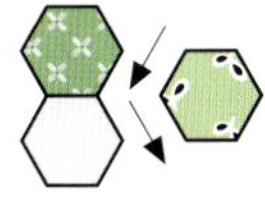

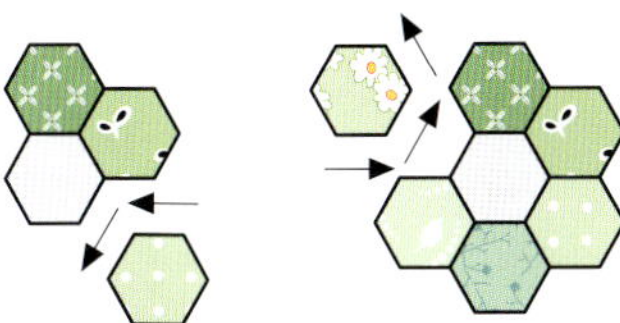

5 Remove the paper templates by carefully cutting away the background fabric behind the appliquéd flower.

6 To add the optional border, sew the shorter strips to opposite sides of the block, pressing the seam allowances toward the strips. Then join the longer strips to the remaining two sides of the block. Press the seam allowances toward the strips.

Block 23
English Paper-Pieced Heart

Materials

1 square, 3" x 3", *each* of 5 assorted light-blue florals

1 square, 6½" x 6½", of black background print

Paper for kites

Optional border:

2 strips, 1½" x 6½"

2 strips, 1½" x 8½"

Block Instructions

1 Refer to "English Paper Piecing" on page 6 when making this block. Using the kite pattern on page 37, trace and cut out five paper kites. Pin a kite template to each blue square and trim the fabric around the kite shape, leaving at least ¼" on all sides for the seam allowance. Baste the blue pieces around the paper kites. Make five.

Make 5.

2 Stitch two kite shapes together, shoulder to toe, as shown. Repeat, reversing the orientation of the two kites as shown. Make one of each unit.

Make 1 of each.

3 Join the two units from step 2 along a short edge. Add the last kite to the bottom to complete the heart.

4 Center the heart on the background square, pin, and hand stitch in place.

5 Remove the paper templates by carefully cutting away the background fabric behind the heart shape.

6 To add the optional border, sew the shorter strips to opposite sides of the block, pressing the seam allowances toward the strips. Then join the longer strips to the remaining two sides of the block. Press the seam allowances toward the strips.

Block 24
Hexagon Vignette

Materials

- 10 squares, 1½" x 1½", of assorted small-scale pink prints
- 1 square, 1½" x 1½", of orange print
- 2 squares, 1½" x 1½", of green print
- 1 square, 1½" x 1½", *each* of 2 different bright prints
- 1 square, 6½" x 6½", of black background fabric
- 11" length of ¼"-wide premade bias tape
- Paper for hexagons

Optional border:

- 2 strips, 1½" x 6½"
- 2 strips, 1½" x 8½"

Block Instructions

1. Refer to "English Paper Piecing" on page 6 when making this block. Using the small hexagon pattern on page 37, trace and cut out 15 paper hexagons. Pin a hexagon template to each 1½" square and trim the fabric around the hexagon shape, leaving at least ¼" on all sides for the seam allowance. Baste the trimmed pieces around the paper hexagons. Make 15.

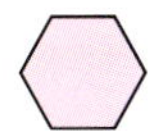 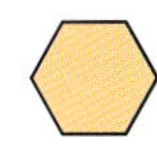 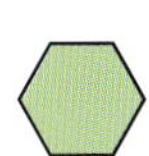 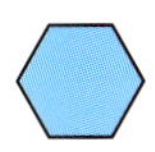

Make 10.   Make 1.   Make 2 of each.

2. Whipstitch one pink hexagon to the orange hexagon. Add a second pink hexagon by whipstitching it first to the pink hexagon already in place, and then whipstitching it to the orange hexagon as indicated by the arrows.

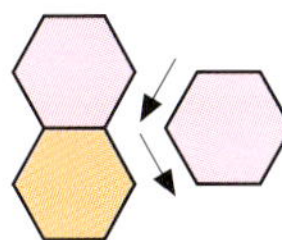

3. Continue to add pink hexagons in a ring around the orange hexagon.

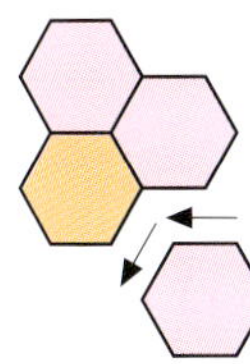

4. When adding the last hexagon to the ring, stitch three sides to the adjoining hexagons as shown.

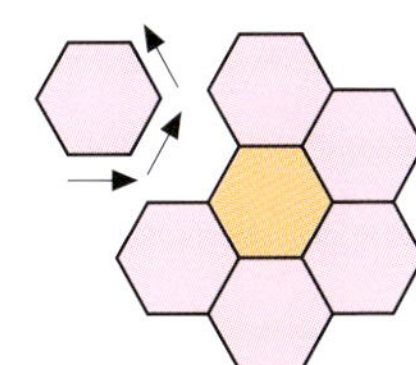 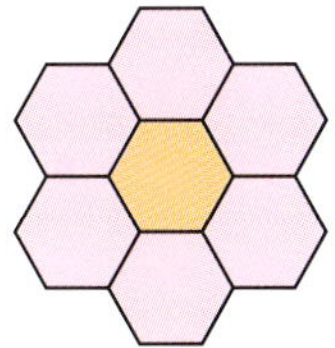

Make 1.

5 Sew one green and two pink hexagons together to form a bud. Make two.

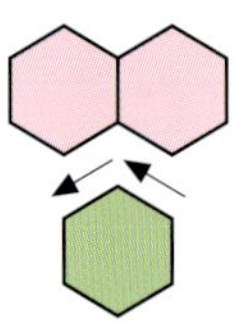

Make 2.

6 Using the photo as a guide, arrange the bias tape in three lengths on the background square (strips are approximately 1", 2", and 6" long). Pin and hand stitch in place. Pin the hexagon flower and buds onto the background, covering the ends of the bias tape, and stitch in place. Pin the two bright hexagons onto the background, and stitch into place.

7 Remove the paper templates by carefully cutting away the background fabric behind each appliquéd shape.

8 To add the optional border, sew the shorter strips to opposite sides of the block, pressing the seam allowances toward the strips. Then join the longer strips to the remaining two sides of the block. Press the seam allowances toward the strips.

Block 25
Daisy Dresden Plate

Materials

20 squares, 2½" x 2½", of assorted red and
   pink prints
1 square, 6½" x 6½", of black background
   fabric
1 square, 5" x 5", of beige print
1 square, 5" x 5", of freezer paper
Template plastic

Optional border:
2 strips, 1½" x 6½"
2 strips, 1½" x 8½"

Block Instructions

1 Trace the small Dresden wedge pattern
on page 37 onto template plastic and cut
out. Place the template on a red or pink
2½" square and trace around the shape.
Cut on the drawn line to make one wedge
shape. Repeat to make a total of 20
wedges.

2 Fold each wedge shape in half, right
sides together, and sew across the wider
end using a ¼" seam allowance. You can
chain piece these seams to speed up the
process and save thread.

 Fold. 

3 Turn each sewn wedge right side out and
use an object with a rounded tip (such as
a knitting needle) to gently push the point
all the way out, creating a blade shape.
Press flat. Make 20.

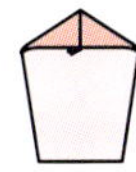 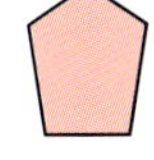

Make 20.

4 Lay out the blades in a ring as shown.

5 Aligning the shoulders of the blades and
using a ¼" seam allowance, sew the
blades together to form the ring. It's OK
if the bottoms of the blades don't align
exactly, as they'll be covered by the center
circle. Press all of the seam allowances in
the same direction.

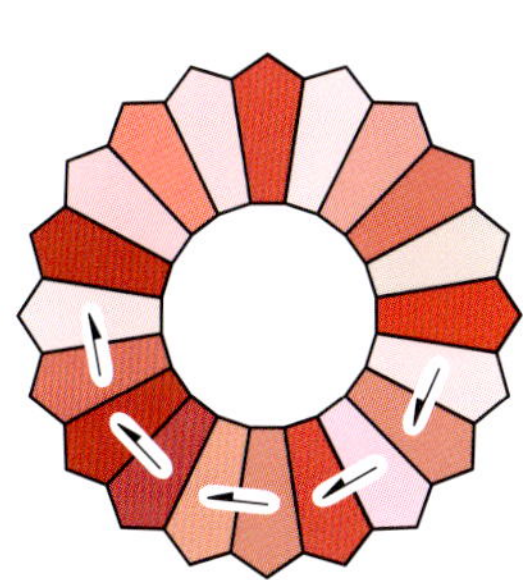

6 Fold the background square in half vertically and horizontally to find the center point. Center the ring of blades on the square and pin in place, keeping the ring as flat as possible. Using either a blanket stitch (by hand or machine) or a slip stitch, sew the pointed outer edge of the ring to the background fabric.

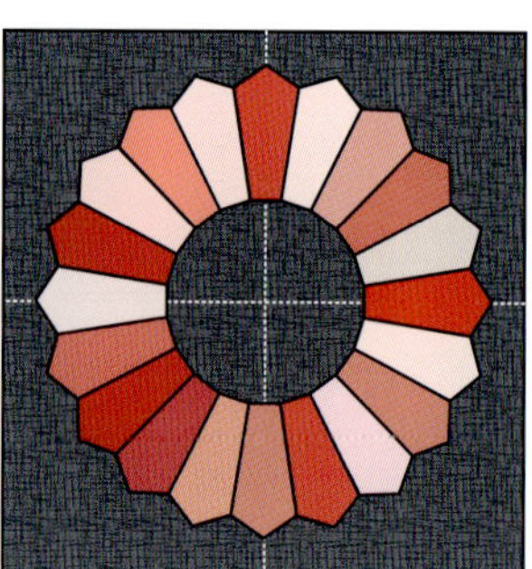

7 Trace the daisy circle pattern on page 37 onto the paper side of the freezer paper and cut out. Using a *dry* iron, press the freezer-paper circle, shiny side down, to the wrong side of the beige square. Cut around the circle, leaving a generous ¼" seam allowance. Using a *dry*, cool iron, gently press the seam allowance over the freezer-paper template.

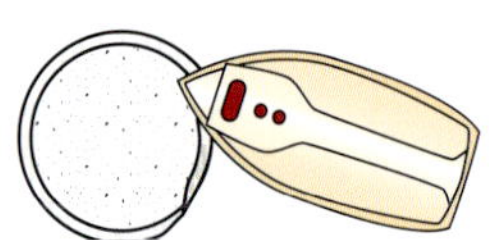

8 Fold the circle into quarters and press lightly with an iron. Unfold and center the circle on the ring, using the pressed lines as a guide. Pin. Using the same stitch that you used in step 6, sew the circle in place.

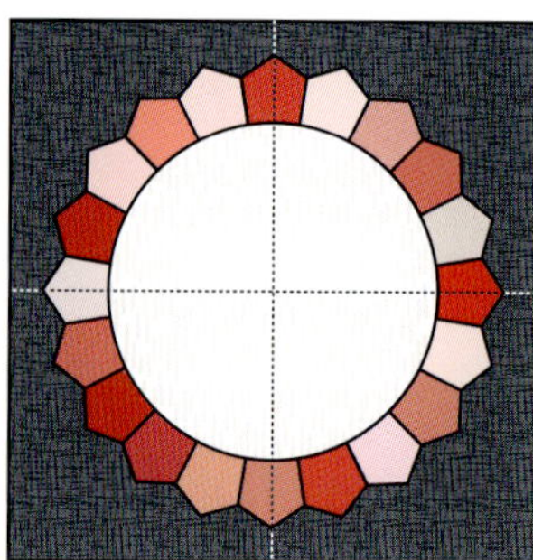

9 On the reverse side of the block, use small, sharp scissors to carefully cut away the background fabric behind the appliquéd circle, and then remove the freezer-paper template.

10 To add the optional border, sew the shorter strips to opposite sides of the block, pressing the seam allowances toward the strips. Then join the longer strips to the remaining two sides of the block. Press the seam allowances toward the strips.

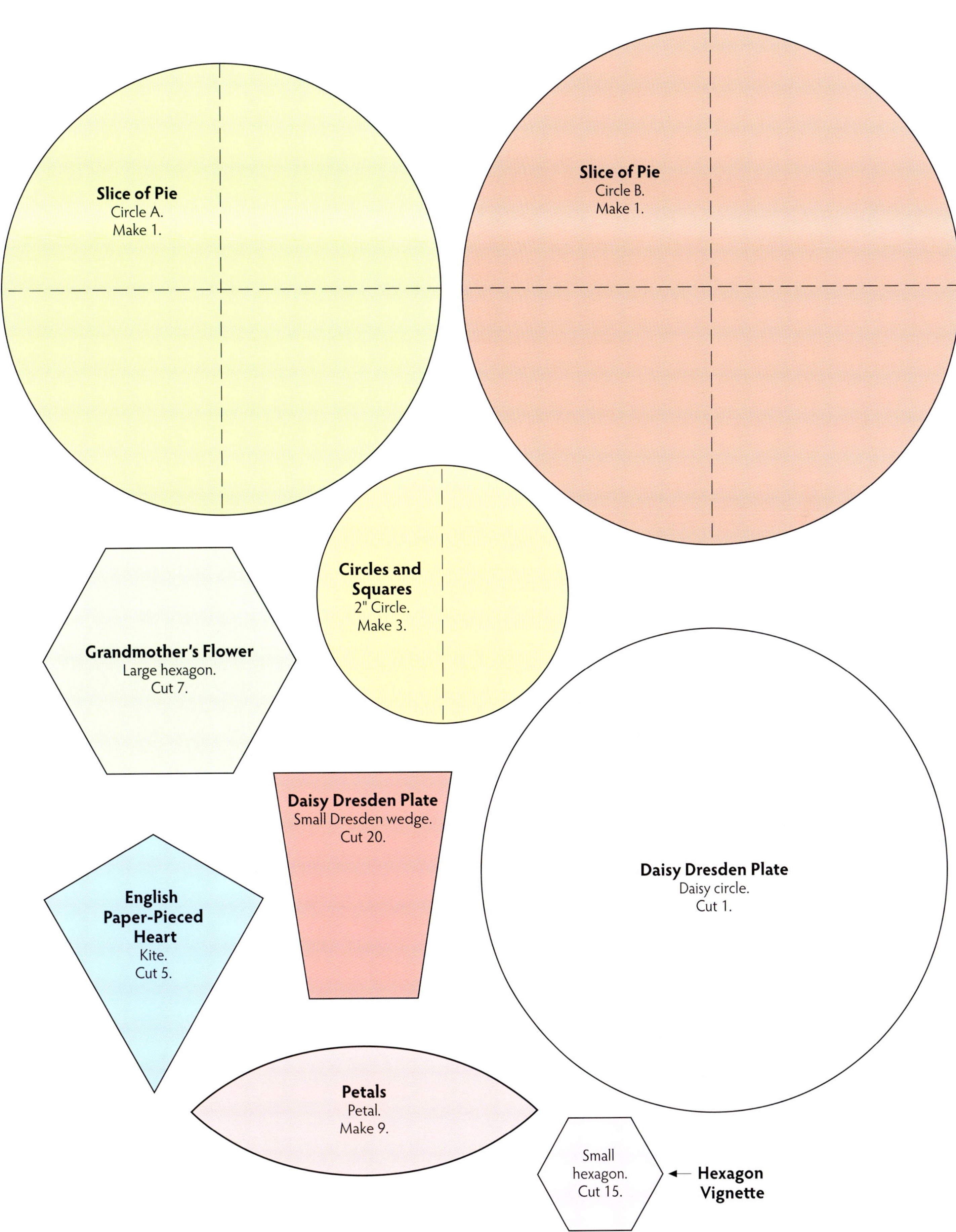

Slice of Pie
Circle A.
Make 1.
Slice of Pie
Circle B.
Make 1.
Circles and Squares
2" Circle.
Make 3.
Grandmother's Flower
Large hexagon.
Cut 7.
Daisy Dresden Plate
Small Dresden wedge.
Cut 20.
Daisy Dresden Plate
Daisy circle.
Cut 1.
English Paper-Pieced Heart
Kite.
Cut 5.
Petals
Petal.
Make 9.
Small hexagon.
Cut 15.
Hexagon Vignette

One-Block Project
Betty's Apron

When I cook, I like to wear an apron because otherwise I wipe my hands on my clothes and end up in a complete mess. This simple half-apron style reminds me of being a small child and spending hours upon hours in my Grandmother Betty's apple-green-and-white 1950s-style kitchen. She wasn't much of a cook, but she was always wearing an apron. Just like Betty's apron, this one has a pocket for your handkerchief and hand cream.

Finished size: 17" x 21" (not including ties)
Block used: Hexagon Vignette (page 33)

Materials

Fat quarters measure 18" x 21".

1 block of your choice

1 fat quarter of floral print for apron

1 fat quarter of black-and-white check for apron ties

1 square, 8½" x 8½", of fabric for pocket lining

Cutting

Follow the cutting directions for the individual block, including the optional border.

From the floral print, cut:

1 rectangle, 17½" x 20½"

From the black-and-white check, cut:

5 strips, 3½" x 20½"

Assembly

1 Assemble the block of your choice as instructed, making sure to add the optional border.

2 Turn under ¼" along the two shorter sides and the bottom edge of the floral rectangle and press. Turn under another ¼" on the same edges and press. Pin the folds in place and then topstitch ⅛" from the edges, pivoting at the corners.

3 Along the top edge of the apron (the unhemmed edge), measure 4" in from each side and make a simple pleat by folding under ½" at each location. The pleats should open toward the sides of the apron. Machine baste along the top edge of each pleat to hold it in place. Press the pleats.

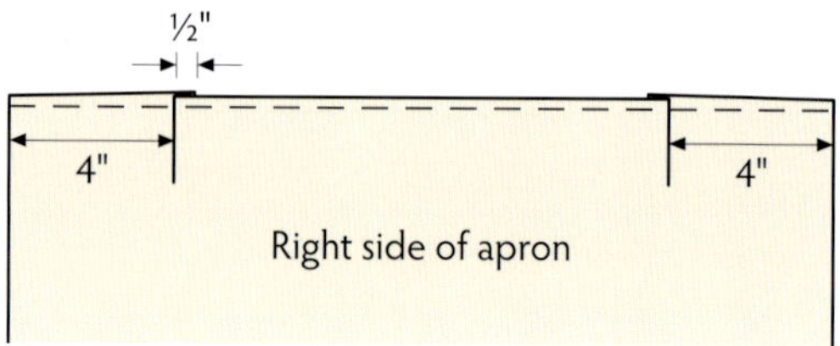

4 Sew the black-and-white strips together end to end to make one long strip. Turn under ¼" on both ends and press. Turn under another ¼" on both ends and press. Pin the folds in place and topstitch along the edge of the folds to form a hem on each end. Fold the strip in half, wrong sides together, and press. Open the strip, turn under ¼" on both of the long edges, and press.

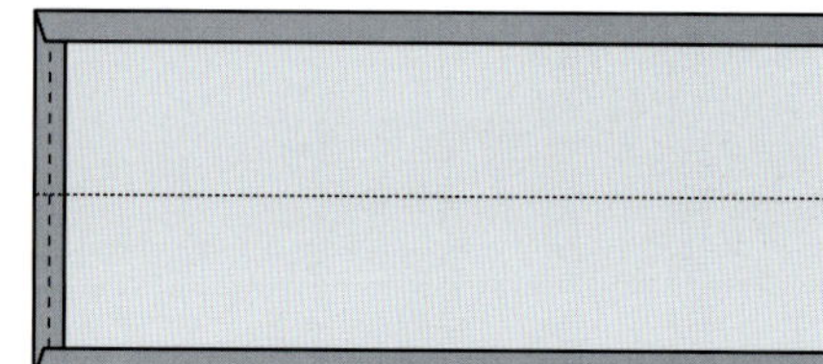

5 Fold the tie in half to find the center point. Fold the apron in half horizontally to find the center point. Aligning the center points, insert the top ½" of the apron into the folded strip and pin in place across the width of the apron. Beginning at one end of the folded tie, stitch near the folded edges along the full length of the tie to close it and attach it to the apron.

6 Sew the prepared patchwork block and the 8½" lining-fabric square right sides together, leaving a 2" opening at the bottom for turning. Clip the corners, turn right side out, and press.

7 Pin the pocket in place on the apron, with the opening for turning at the bottom. The exact placement of the pocket is a matter of personal preference; mine is at a jaunty angle to allow easy access by my right hand. You might want to try on your apron to make sure the pocket location suits you. Stitch the pocket onto the apron, backstitching at the beginning and end of the seam to hold the pocket securely in place. Don't forget to leave the top edge open, or the pocket will be just a patch!

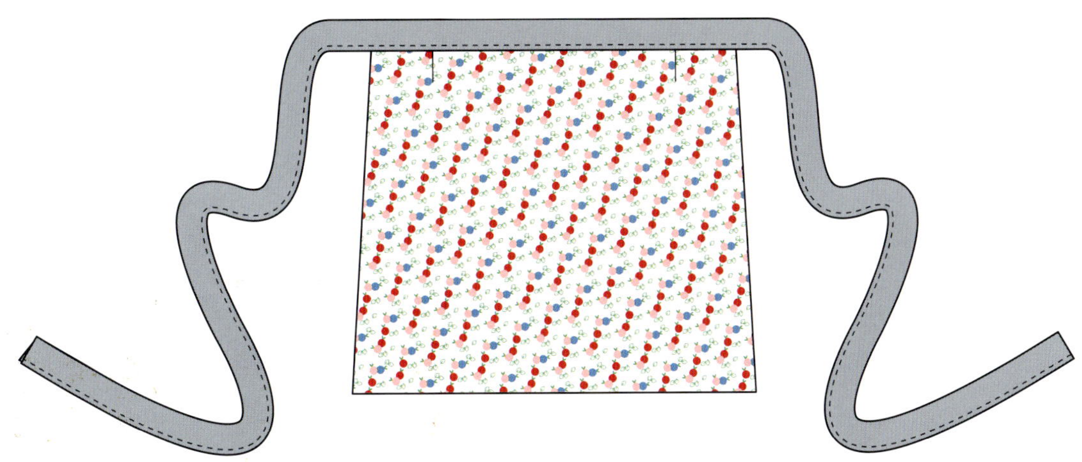

One-Block Project
Keep-Safe Drawstring Bag

A huge project tote is great, but if you don't have a smaller bag to keep inside of it, all of your little bits and bobs (such as a needle case, scissors, and thread) can become lost in the bottom of the tote. This drawstring bag will keep those little notions close at hand. And it's so easy to whip together, you may find yourself making multiples!

Finished size: 8½" x 8½" (not including drawstring casing)
Block used: Framed Diamond (page 30)

Materials

- 1 block of your choice
- 2 squares, 8½" x 8½", of fabric for lining
- 1 square, 8½" x 8½", of fabric for bag back
- 2 strips, 2½" x 8½", of fabric for ribbon casing
- 60" length of ribbon, ¾" wide

Assembly

1. Assemble the block of your choice as instructed, making sure to add the optional border.

2. Using a generous ¼" seam allowance, sew the lining squares right sides together around three edges, leaving the top unstitched and a 2" opening in the bottom for turning later.

Leave open for turning.

3. Turn under ¼" on both ends of a 2½" x 8½" strip and press. Turn under another ¼" on both ends and press. Pin the folds in place and topstitch along the edge of the folds to form a hem on each end. Repeat with the second ribbon-casing strip. Fold both strips in half lengthwise, wrong sides together, and press.

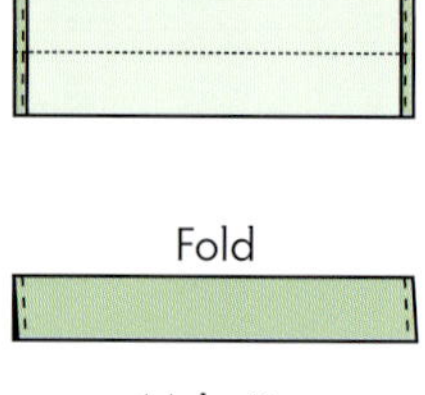

Fold

Make 2.

4. With right sides up, lay out the the block and the square for the bag back. Center, pin, and attach the raw edges of the strips to the top edge of the block and the square, using a scant ¼" seam allowance to form drawstring channels.

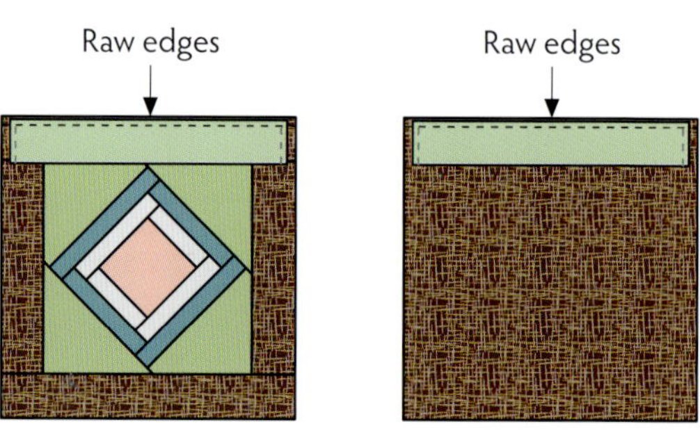

5 With right sides together, use a ¼" seam allowance and sew the block and the bag back together along three edges, being careful not to catch the channels in the side seams. Leave the top edge open. Turn right sides out and press.

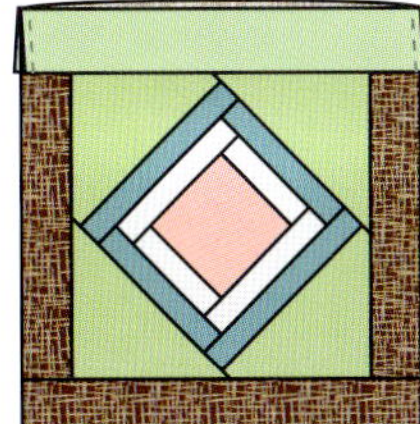

Leave top edge open.

6 With right sides together, insert the outside of the bag into the lining. The drawstring channels should be between the lining and the bag. Pin around the top of the bag and use a ¼" seam allowance to sew the outside of the bag and the lining together around the top.

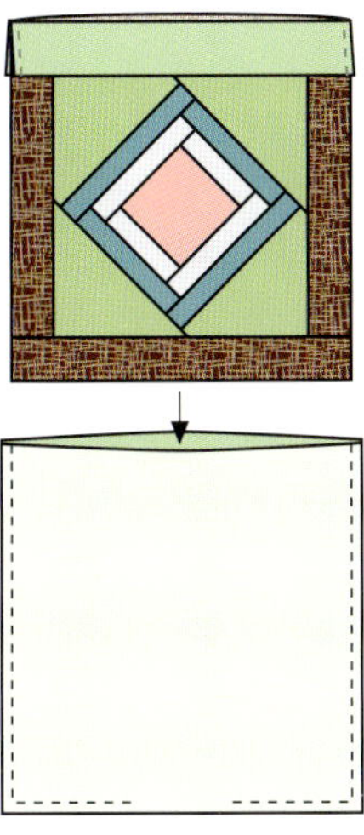

Insert bag into lining.

Stitch together around
top edge.

7 Turn the bag right side out through the opening in the lining, and then stitch the opening closed by hand or machine. Push the lining into the bag and press the bag well.

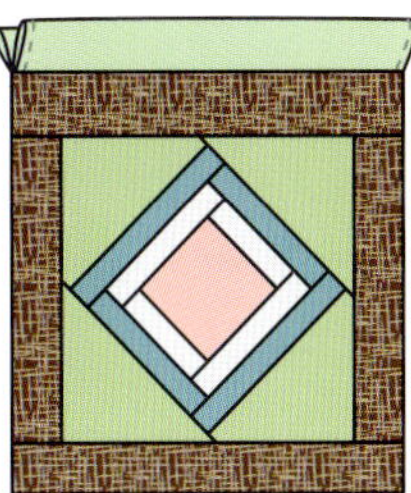

8 Cut the ribbon into two equal lengths and thread one length through each drawstring channel. Either knot or stitch the ends of the ribbon together to secure.

Two-Block Project
Field of Daisies Quilt

I originally designed this quilt to be used on picnics, having a romantic idea that it would look lovely lying in a summer meadow, surrounded by sweetly scented wild-flowers. The large circles of the daisy centers could act as place mats for delicious home-baked breads and cakes, salads, and sandwiches.

In reality, as I live in the United Kingdom where the summer is mostly rainy and a little chilly, this quilt is more likely to be used as a shelter from a sudden downpour. Maybe you're luckier with the weather than I am!

Pieced by Katy Jones and machine quilted by Chris Marriage

Finished size: 63½" x 63½"
Blocks used: Grandmother's Flower (page 31) and Daisy Dresden Plate (page 35, enlarged)

Materials

Yardage is based on 42"-wide fabric unless otherwise noted. Fat quarters measure 18" x 21".

3½ yards of gray print for block
   backgrounds*

2 yards *total* of assorted pink and red prints
   for blades**

9 fat quarters of assorted light neutral prints for
   flower centers

½ yard *total* of assorted green prints for
   hexagons**

⅝ yard of green fabric for binding

4⅜ yards of fabric for backing

72" x 72" piece of batting

Lightweight cardstock

Paper for hexagons

Template plastic

Spray starch (optional)

**This fabric must have a usable width of at least 43".*

***Scraps work well for this project, and I encourage you to use as many prints as possible. Each pink or red scrap needs to be at least 3" x 4¼", or you can use 8 fat quarters. Each green scrap needs to be at least 2½" x 2½".*

I used newsprint or text-print fabrics in neutral colors. Choose nine fabrics that are similar in color and tone to give your quilt a cohesive look when they are pieced together for the flower centers.

Cutting

From the gray print, cut:
5 strips, 21½" x 43"; cut into 9 squares,
   21½" x 21½"

From the assorted pink and red prints, cut:
180 rectangles, 3" x 4¼"

From *each* of the 9 neutral fat quarters, cut:
1 strip, 6½" x 16½"
1 square, 10½" x 10½"
1 rectangle, 6½" x 10½"

From the assorted green prints, cut:
64 squares, 2½" x 2½"

From the green fabric for binding, cut:
7 strips, 2½" x 42"

Assembly

1 Refer to "English Paper Piecing" on page 6 when making this quilt. Trace the large Dresden wedge pattern on page 45 onto template plastic and cut out. Place the template on a pink or red rectangle and trace around the shape. Cut on the drawn line to make one wedge shape. Repeat to make a total of 180 wedges. Use the large hexagon pattern on page 37 to trace and cut out 64 paper hexagons. Pin a hexagon template to each green 2½" square and trim the fabric around the hexagon, leaving at least ¼" on all sides for the seam allowance. Baste the green pieces around the paper hexagons. Make 64 total.

2 Following the instructions in steps 2–6 on pages 35 and 36 for the Daisy Dresden Plate block, make nine large rings and hand or machine appliqué each ring onto a gray square.

3 Using pieces from three different neutral fabrics, sew a 6½" x 10½" rectangle to the top edge of a 10½" square. Press the seam allowances toward the square. Sew a 6½" x 16½" strip to the right side of the unit. Press the seam allowances toward the strip to complete one pieced block. Repeat to make a total of nine pieced blocks.

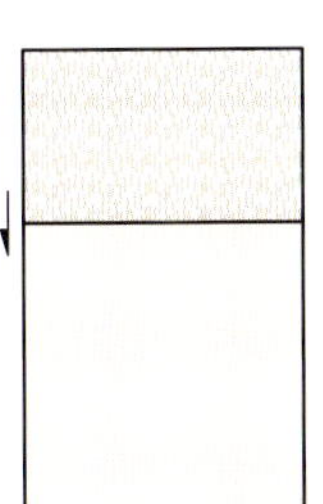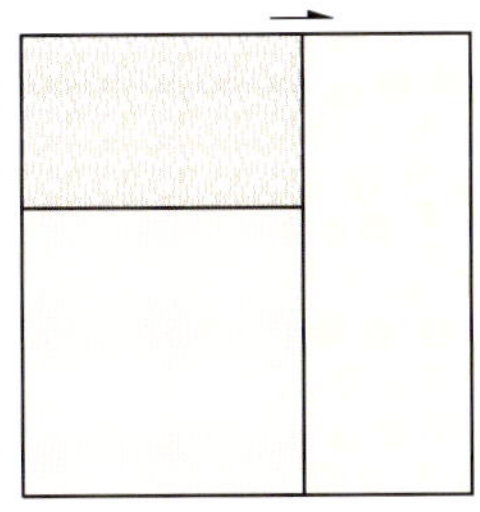

Make 9.

4 Trace the quarter-circle template from page 45 onto cardstock four times, aligning edges as indicated on the template, to form a 14½"-diameter circle. Cut the circle out on the drawn line. Using this as a guide, cut a circle from a pieced block, *adding ½" for the seam allowance* all the way around. Using a *dry* iron, gently press

the seam allowance over the circle template. You may wish to use a little starch to stiffen the edges.

5 Carefully remove the template and pin the circle onto the center of a ring from step 2, ensuring that the circle covers all the raw inner edges of the ring. Pin well, and then machine or hand appliqué into place. Repeat to make a total of nine Daisy Dresden Plate blocks.

▼ Hand vs. Machine

Hand-appliqué stitches are more time consuming than machine stitches, but they are also less obvious. To give your quilt a better, more professional finish, I encourage you to give hand stitching a try.

6 Lay out the blocks in three rows of three blocks each. Sew the blocks into rows. Press the seam allowances in opposite directions from row to row to create opposing seams. Sew the rows together and press the seam allowances in one direction. Press the entire quilt top well.

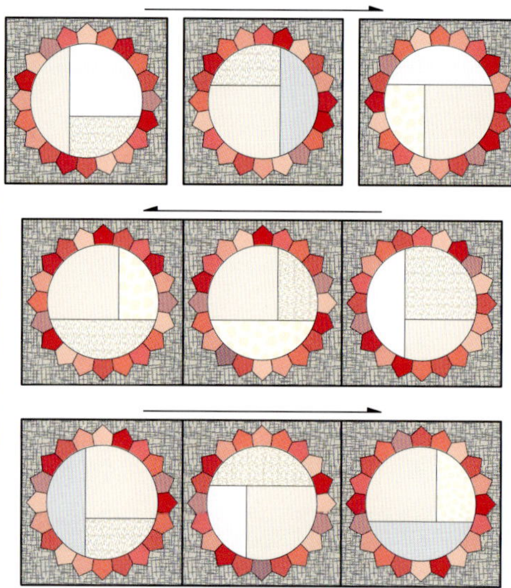

7 Following the instructions in steps 2–4 on page 31 for the Grandmother's Flower block, use the basted green hexagons to make four hexagon flowers. The remaining hexagons will be added as scattered petals throughout the quilt top.

8 Using the quilt photo as a guide, pin the hexagon flowers and petals into place on the background fabric. Position the flowers where the seams of four Daisy Dresden Plate blocks intersect. Hand appliqué the flowers and petals into place. On the reverse side of the quilt, use small, sharp scissors to carefully cut away the background fabric behind the appliqués, and then carefully remove the paper templates.

9 Cut the length of the backing fabric in half to create two 78"-long pieces. Sew the two pieces together side by side using a ½" seam allowance. Press the seam allowances in one direction.

10 Layer the quilt top, batting, and backing; baste the layers together. Quilt as desired or take your quilt top to a professional long-arm machine quilter.

11 Bind the edges using the 2½"-wide green strips.

▼ **Quilting Ideas**

The quilt shown was professionally quilted on a long-arm machine in an allover repeating hexagon pattern, giving the center of the large daisies a particularly sunflower-like appearance. Another idea would be to quilt a spiral in the center of each large daisy, and then echo quilt around the petals to create a series of zigzagging ripples.

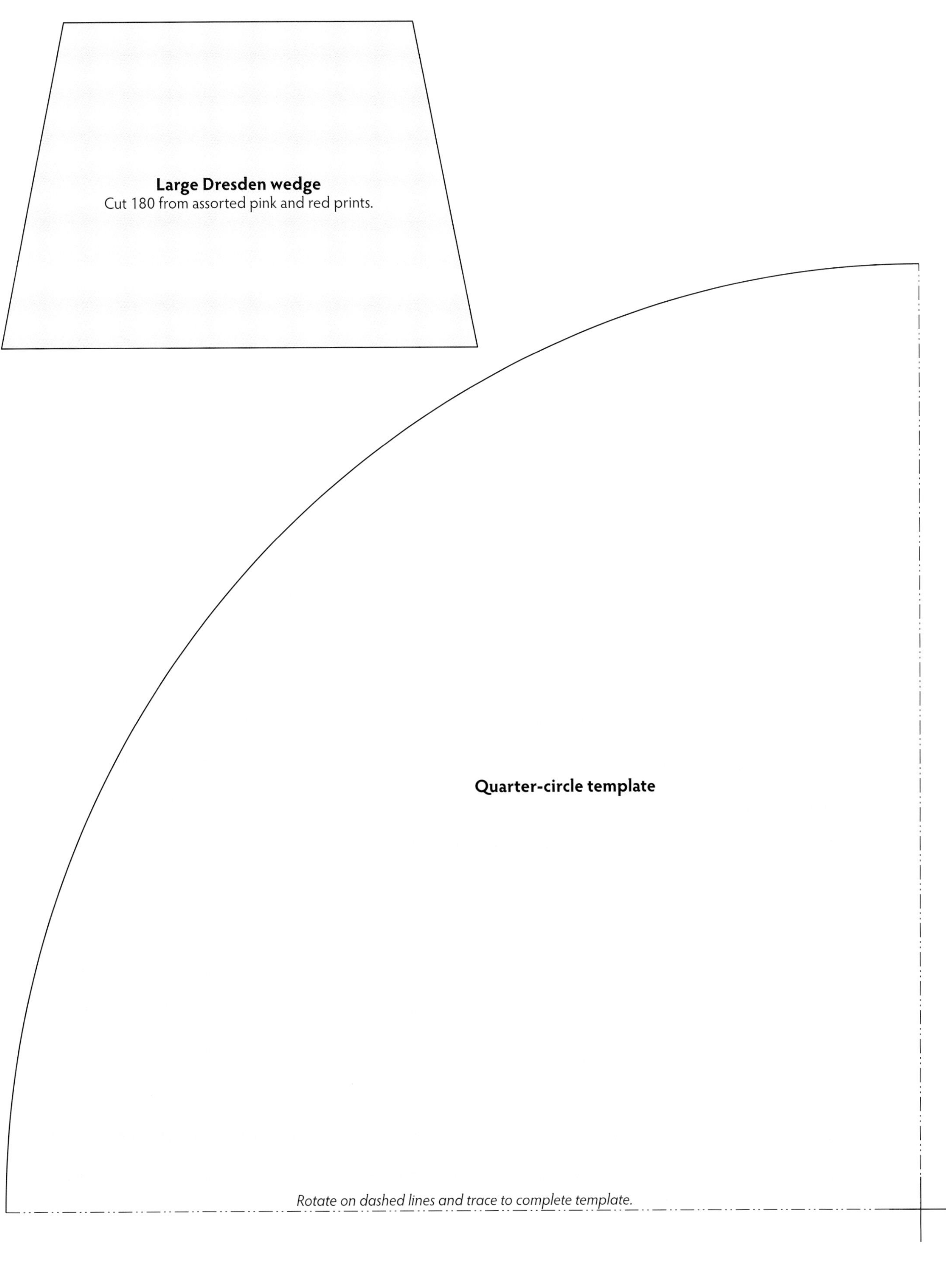

Large Dresden wedge
Cut 180 from assorted pink and red prints.

Quarter-circle template

Rotate on dashed lines and trace to complete template.

Two-Block Project
Love You Baby Quilt

This little quilt is based on two appliquéd blocks. Four blocks of the first design combine in a center medallion, while 16 blocks of the second design join to make the outer border. The quilt is designed to use up lots of small scraps, so this would be an ideal memory quilt featuring precious clothes from baby's first year.

Pieced and quilted by Katy Jones

Finished size: 30½" x 30½"
Blocks used: Petals (page 21) and English Paper-Pieced Heart (page 32)

Materials

Yardage is based on 42"-wide fabric unless otherwise noted. Fat quarters measure 18" x 21".

⅞ yard *total* of assorted medium-value prints for hearts and petals

¾ yard *total* of assorted light-value prints for Petals block backgrounds

⅝ yard of black print for Heart block backgrounds and binding

1 fat quarter of gray print for Heart block borders

1 fat quarter of blue print for inner border

1¼ yards of fabric for backing

38" x 38" piece of batting

⅞ yard of paper-backed fusible web

Paper for kites

Cutting

From the assorted medium-value prints, cut:
20 squares, 3" x 3"
144 rectangles, 1½" x 3½"

From the assorted light-value prints, cut:
144 squares, 2½" x 2½"

From the black print, cut:
3 strips, 2½" x 42"
4 squares, 6½" x 6½"

From the gray print, cut:
8 strips, 1½" x 6½"
8 strips, 1½" x 8½"

From the blue print, cut:
2 strips, 1½" x 16½"
2 strips, 1½" x 18½"

Assembly

1 Follow the instructions in steps 1–6 on page 32 for the Heart block to make four blocks, substituting medium-value prints for the light-blue florals in the pattern. Use the gray strips to add the optional border to the blocks.

2 Follow the instructions in steps 1–3 on page 21 for the Petals block to make 16 blocks, substituting light-value prints for the beige prints in the pattern and substituting medium prints for the bright prints. Do *not* add the optional border to the blocks.

3 Sew the four Heart blocks into two rows as shown. Press the seam allowances as indicated by the arrows to create opposing seams. Sew the rows together and press the seam allowances in one direction to complete the quilt center.

4 Stitch the blue 16½"-long strips to the top and bottom of the quilt center. Press the seam allowances toward the strips. Stitch

the blue 18½"-long strips to the sides of
the quilt center. Press the seam allowances
toward the strips.

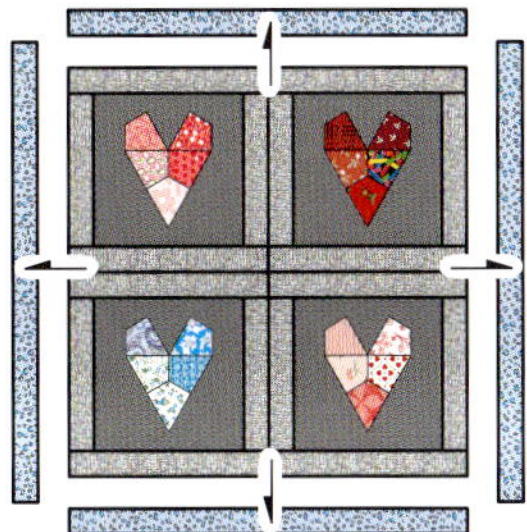

5 Sew three Petals blocks together in a
row, rotating the blocks so that the petals
alternate direction from block to block.
Press the seam allowances open to reduce
bulk. Repeat to make a second row, orient-
ing the blocks as in the first row. Press the
seam allowances open to reduce bulk.
Keeping the rows in the same orientation,
sew these border rows to the top and
bottom of the quilt center. Press the seam
allowances toward the quilt center. Lay the
quilt top on a flat surface or design wall
and arrange two vertical rows of five Petals
blocks *each*, rotating the blocks so that
the petals alternate direction from block to
block. Check to see that the petal orientation is correct where the vertical rows meet
the horizontal rows. When your blocks are
oriented correctly, stitch them together into
two vertical border strips. Press the seam
allowances open to reduce bulk. Sew
the border strips to the sides of the quilt.
Press the seam allowances toward the quilt
center.

6 Layer the quilt top, batting, and backing;
baste the layers together. Quilt as desired
or take your quilt top to a professional
long-arm machine quilter.

7 Bind the edges using the 2½"-wide
black strips.

▼ Quilting Ideas

The quilt shown was quilted in a simple diagonal grid that follows the corners of the blocks in
the outer border. I used a neutral cotton thread
that blends well with the different colors in the
fabrics. Grid quilting like this makes the quilt
quite stiff, which is perfect for a wall hanging or
for any quilt that you want to display flat.

About the Author

Katy Jones is a British quilter, blogger, author, wife, and mummy who first started quilting in 2008 with the gentle encouragement of a friend. Her first quilt was somewhat of a disaster, since she made it up as she went along and hoped for the best. "The best" didn't really happen, but the quilt was used and loved and it started her on a path of obsession that has culminated in this book. In 2010, Katy cofounded the popular digital quilting eMagazine *Fat Quarterly*, and she regularly teaches patchwork and quilting workshops, hoping she can convert the whole world to the joy of quilting.

You can visit ImAGingerMonkey.blogspot.co.uk to follow Katy's adventures in quilting, patchwork, and all things fabric.

Be sure to check out Katy's first book, *25 Patchwork Quilt Blocks* (Martingale, 2013). She has also been published in a number of other books on patchwork and quilting, including *Modern Quilts from the Blogging Universe* (Martingale, 2012).

Acknowledgments and Suggested Sites

Thank you to the following manufacturers and shop owners for their help with supplying tools and fabrics:

> Aurifil thread
(www.Aurifil.com)

> Robert Kaufman Fabrics
(RobertKaufman.com)

> Timeless Treasures Fabrics
(TTFabrics.com)

> Amitié Textiles
(Amitie.com.au)

> Lucie at Summersville
(Etsy.com/Shop/Summersville)

> Brenda at Pink Castle Fabrics
(PinkCastleFabrics.com)

> Becca at Sew Me a Song
(Etsy.com/Shop/SewMeaSong)

I hope you will be inspired by the following websites and blogs!

> SewMamaSew.com

> ThreadBias.com

> TheModernQuiltGuild.com

> InColorOrder.com

> SarahFielke.com

> Quiltville.blogspot.com

> verykerryberry.blogspot.co.uk

> FilmintheFridge.com

> RedPepperQuilts.com

> TheHappyZombie.com